GOOD GOVERNANCE AND POVERTY ALLEVIATION

About the Authors

D. Rajasekhar is Professor and Head at the Centre for Decentralisation and Development, Institute for Social and Economic Change (ISEC), Bangalore. His areas of specialisation are decentralisation, micro-finance, social protection for the unorganised workers and rural development. He has published 17 books and over 60 research articles in various journals of repute and edited books. He is currently engaged in a major research project on 'Improving Institutions for Pro-Poor Growth', undertaken in collaboration with Oxford University and London School of Economics, UK.

K.G. Gayathridevi is Associate Professor at the Centre for Decentralisation and Development, ISEC, Bangalore. Her areas of interest are gender concerns in decentralisation, people's organisations, promotion of economic enterprises, sericulture, social mobility and child labour. She has published a number of research papers in various reputed journals. As a Research Fellow at the Department of Sociology at University of Glasgow in 1995, she undertook research on social mobility and scheduled castes. She is currently involved in a research study on 'Fuelling Fire or Dampening Flames? Conflict Management by Grama Panchayats in Karnataka'.

Sachidananda Satapathy is an ICSSR Doctoral student at the Centre for Decentralisation and Development, ISEC, Bangalore. He is currently working on 'Youth Transition and Local Organisations: Employment Generation Programmes in Orissa' for his doctoral dissertation. He has published two books on 'Orissa Vision 2020: Towards Building a New and Modern Orissa' and 'Youth Vision 2020: Towards Building an India of Our Choice'. He represented the country at the Global Round Table on Youth Citizenship at London in 2004, and was awarded Infosys Young Achiever Award in 2005.

GOOD GOVERNANCE and POVERTY ALLEVIATION

A Study of SGSY Programme

D Rajasekhar
K G Gayathridevi
Sachidananda Satapathy

Centre for Decentralisation and Development
Institute for Social and Economic Change, Bangalore

CONCEPT PUBLISHING COMPANY, NEW DELHI-110059

Cataloging in Publication Data—DK
Courtesy: D.K. Agencies (P) Ltd. <docinfo@dkagencies.com>

Rajasekhar, D. (Durgam), 1960-
Good governance and poverty alleviation : a study of SGSY programme / D. Rajasekhar, K.G. Gayathridevi, Sachidananda Satapathy.
p. cm.
Study conducted at Betul and Chhattarpur districts of Madhya Pradesh, India.
Includes bibliographical references (p.)
Includes index.
ISBN 13: 9788180694820
ISBN 10: 8180694828

1. Swarnjayanti Gram Swarozgar Yojana (India).—Evaluation. 2. Rural poor—Employment—Government policy—India—Madhya Pradesh. 3. Self-employed—Government policy—India—Madhya Pradesh. 4. Rural development projects—India—Madhya Pradesh —Citizen participation. 5. Poverty—Government policy—India—Madhya Pradesh. I. Gayathridevi, K. G., joint author. II. Satapathy, Sachidananda, joint author. III. Title.

DDC 339.460 954 3 22

ISBN-13:978-81-8069-482-0
ISBN-10:81-8069-482-8

First Published 2007

Published and Printed by
Ashok Kumar Mittal
Concept Publishing Company,
A/15-16, Commercial Block, Mohan Garden,
New Delhi-110059 (INDIA)

Phones: 25351460, 25351794
Fax: 091-11-25357103
Email: publishing@conceptpub.com

Preface

Poverty in India has a strong gender dimension. In order to reduce poverty, interventions should aim not only at the improvement of material condition of women but also lead to their empowerment. The government has been formulating and implementing policies and programmes for women development and empowerment. A review of these policies and programmes and the successful programmes of civil society organisations, together with political mobilisation of women, have resulted in a number of policy and programmatic changes. Of them, an important change was the shift in targeting strategy from 'individual beneficiaries' to 'Self-help Groups (SHGs) of women involved in micro-finance'.

SHGs are considered to be having great potential in building social capital and promoting collective action and achieving equitable, effective and sustainable delivery of financial and other development services to the poor women. This has influenced the governments at the Central and State levels, bilateral and multilateral agencies to formulate programmes for women's development and empowerment through SHGs since 1990s. One such programme, viz., Swarnajayanti Gram Swarozgar Yojana (SGSY), which has been initiated by the Department of Rural Development and implemented through Panchayat Raj Institutions (PRIs) all over the country, is important because of its size.

This programme adopted the strategy of micro-finance as an instrument of women development and empowerment. By initiating micro-finance and other activities through SHGs, the SGSY programme has aimed at improving and sustaining access to credit among poor women for meeting their consumption and production needs, and resources from the line department and local elected bodies. The design of this programme has specified functions to different organisations such as PRIs, NGOs and SHGs. Such assignment of functions reflects the global and Indian thinking on promoting good governance in poverty reduction programmes.

The new good governance paradigm suggests pluralisation of state for development. This paradigm suggests that development challenges should be addressed collaboratively by building partnerships among the State, market and civil society. This paradigm is recommended for all the developing countries because good development outcomes can be achieved through such a collaboration, and adoption of good governance principles such as participation, transparency and accountability. The linkages and relations among different actors are to be harmonised through capacity building and co-ordination. The evidence, however, demonstrates that this multiplicity of actors (i.e., pluralisation of state) has created confusion and some conflict within the local institutional landscape. These multiple local organisations have rarely proved able to fully embrace their mandated functions, their comparative advantage is unclear and the nature of their working relationships is often ambiguous.

This volume explores the links between good governance incorporated in the SGSY programme and poverty alleviation in the specific context of Madhya Pradesh by addressing the following questions. What were the processes followed in the implementation of SGSY programme? Did the programme succeed in mobilising the people in the formation of SGSY groups, and in planning and implementation? What was the participation of the people in savings contribution, and borrowing from the groups? What were the linkages between the groups formed under the programme, on the one hand, and decentralised government, banks, etc., on the other? Was the right kind of synergy and harmony among multiple players generated?

The evidence presented in this volume shows that participatory processes followed in the social mobilisation and formation of groups were not qualitative. Participation of the people was not widespread in the formation of groups, formulation of rules and regulations, meetings and savings contributions. Factors such as widespread poverty, systems and procedures adopted in the groups, lack of incentives, inappropriate design and interference from village elite/influential persons adversely affected participation of women in SHGs. The limited participation of the people in the programme meant that the performance of the group was affected. Further, this also led to the tendencies of elite capture.

Limited participation in savings contribution meant that members did not have sufficient savings to borrow for meeting urgent consumption credit needs, and for production. Small amounts of savings contributed by women members also meant that vulnerability remained the outstanding problem for the poor. The differential amounts of savings contributed by members and savings linked to credit together implied that those having better economic capacity to save were in an advantageous position to borrow from the group and corner the benefits. This also implies the 'elite capture'.

The analysis on participation of members in credit activities and undertaking of income generation activities shows that the programme had not succeeded in generating viable and locally suitable IGA. In both homogenous and heterogeneous groups, it was the influential groups of households which cornered the benefits. But most often, the loan amount was invested upon already existing economic activities. For those who really thought of starting a new IGA, there were problems of skill acquisition and supply of inputs like raw materials. In the absence of linkages between groups, GP and line departments, collective mobilisation of people to identify economic activities was not even attempted.

Thus, participation meant costs for the poor. The SGSY programme has had limited success in explaining the benefits of the programme to the members, and convincing them that benefits would outweigh the costs of participation in the long-run. The net result was either dismally low levels of participation, or exit of members from the programme or defunct status of the groups.

The analysis of linkages among key development actors shows that there was a considerable bureaucratic control over the entire implementation process. Although theory places heavy emphasis upon state and society linkages as being excellent catalyst for development, and despite the programme envisaging it in principle, it had not yet successfully achieved the objective. Complementarity is expected to enhance sustainable synergy and development. However, the field data do not support all this. First of all, PRIs could not undertake the task of establishing linkages with banks and other institutions. The PRIs themselves have not yet been established firmly and independently as democratic bodies with political, administrative and fiscal powers suitably devolved. Second, the functioning of the groups, being least transparent has encouraged sufficient criticism and led to suspicions about their accountability. Third, although SGSY is open to all, the groups were formed mainly for women. This implies that the development and empowerment of women is challenging, given their illiteracy, restrictions on mobility and feminisation of poverty. Thus, it may take a long time for women to develop through their SHGs; we need to be patient.

The book reaches an important conclusion which is very relevant for theory as well as policy. The design of SGSY programme is good as it seeks further decentralisation in the country and incorporates good governance principles. However, the programme implementation has suffered on account of a number of problems such as inadequate functional assignment, intergovernmental transfers leading to disincentives and unfavourable conditions for income earning through micro-finance initiatives. Thus, bureaucratic attitude, limited decentralisation, lack of minimum development of areas and people contribute to the inability to follow good governance principles and decentralisation for income earning through employment generation.

Acknowledgements

This book is the revised and expanded version of our research project on "Good Governance and Poverty Alleviation: A Study of SGSY Programme" undertaken at the Institute for Social and Economic Change (ISEC), Bangalore. We thank Prof. Gopal K. Kadekodi, the then Director, for his support and encouragement in undertaking this research project.

Our heartfelt thanks are due to Professors V.M. Rao and Abdul Aziz for their critical comments and useful suggestions on the study. In fact, it is their feedback and encouraging words that motivated us to work on the project report to bring it out as a publication. When the results of the study were presented in a seminar at ISEC, several colleagues provided useful comments. We thank all of them. Our sincere thanks are due to Mr. V.S. Parthasarathy for his editorial work and excellent copy-editing of the project report as well as the manuscript.

Our colleagues at the Centre for Decentralisation and Development have always lent a helping hand in the pursuit of our research objectives. In particular, we would like to thank Ms. R. Manjula for not only providing critical comments when the work was presented in seminars, but also for her help and support at various stages of the preparation of the manuscript. We are extremely indebted to her. We thank Ms. Damini Masand, who was associated with the project as a researcher for a brief period in the initial months, for her assistance, especially, in the translation of qualitative data from Hindi.

The research project has used some of the data collected for the project on "Roles of Rural Local Organisations in Development Projects". A special thanks to Dr. Ruth Alsop and Prof. Govinda Rao for their constant support and encouragement in undertaking this project. In the collection of data for this project from Madhya Pradesh, ISEC collaborated with Samarthan, Bhopal. We are thankful to all the staff from Samarthan and Dr. Surendar Jena, in particular, for their help.

Bangalore

D Rajasekhar
K G Gayathridevi
Sachidananda Satapathy

Contents

List of Annexes, Boxes, Charts, Figures and Tables

ANNEXES

BOX

CHARTS

FIGURE

TABLES

1

Introduction

Notwithstanding several efforts by the government during the post independence period, poverty and deprivation continue to be major problems in the country. The government noted that continued deprivation and inequality were the result of poor governance in the country (GoI 2002c). It was also noted that the governance would be good if policies and programmes were equitable, transparent, non-discriminatory, socially sensitive, participatory and accountable to the people. A close relationship was, therefore, seen between good governance and the success of anti-poverty programmes. Against this background, this study analyses the performance of SGSY programme, a major anti-poverty initiative by the Indian government, to examine the extent to which good governance principles have been adopted into the programme and whether these principles have had any impact on the success of the programme.

Poverty in India

Poverty is a concept that describes "the general condition of people who are badly off and encompasses many aspects of want and disadvantages" (Chambers 1988:3). However, what precisely are these wants and disadvantages is always debated. Very frequently, poverty is related to inadequate incomes (poverty line). The conventional approach concentrates on income and/or consumption of the household to describe poverty as the inability of certain sections of the society to obtain income to meet the basic necessities. Dreze and Sen (1989:15) describe poverty as a severe failure of basic capabilities. In their approach, a distinction has been made between 'ends' (capabilities) and 'means' (low incomes or other causal antecedents of failures in basic capabilities). Chambers (1988 and 1995) criticises that the above do not directly consider the perceptions of the 'actors' themselves who may have a different understanding of deprivation and their own priorities. He suggests that five clusters of disadvantages (lack of assets, physical weakness, isolation, vulnerability and powerlessness) characterise the poor in rural areas. The poor themselves perceive that there are three priorities, namely, survival, security and self-respect; the last being their highest priority (Chambers 1988).

Based on the poverty line approach[1], it is estimated that 26.1 per cent of the country's population (or 260.1 million people) lived below the poverty line in 1999-2000. While the proportion of the poor in rural areas was 27 per cent (193.2 million), it was 23.6 per cent (67 million) in urban areas[2].

During the post-independence period, poverty trends seem to have proceeded in three distinct phases. First, the period from the early 1950s to the mid-1970s was characterised by fluctuations in poverty without any clear trend in either direction. Second, the incidence (severity and depth) of poverty steadily declined during the period 1971 to 1990. Third, from the late 1980s, poverty appears to have entered into a new phase of fluctuations[3] probably due to macro-economic reforms introduced in 1991[4]. There are, however, contradicting views on the impact of reforms on poverty (Bhalla 2002; Dev 2002). The recent evidence suggests that the proportion of population living below the poverty line declined after the reform process was initiated in 1991. But the fact that even after five decades of planning, a significant proportion of the population continues to live below poverty line. Further, a decline in the poverty level was not uniform across the states and social groups. The recent papers by Krishna (2003), (Krishna *et al*, 2003 and 2004) show interesting dynamics behind poverty reduction in India. It is not that all the poor who managed to cross the poverty line could hope to remain above the poverty levels. This indicates that the past attempts aimed at poverty alleviation had not succeeded or that altogether different sets of strategies were needed.

The incidence of poverty varies both across the states, and within each of the states. According to income poverty statistics, the poor are concentrated in central and eastern states of India. If poverty is seen from the perspective of non-material deprivation, it spreads to many other states. For instance, Tamil Nadu, Andhra Pradesh and Karnataka, which are better off in terms of income, are worse-off in terms of human development and gender development indices[5].

Poverty has ethnic, caste and gender dimensions. Fifty per cent of the tribals belong to the category of poor. They also suffer from non-material deprivation such as high illiteracy and dropout rates. Dalits (persons belonging to depressed castes) account for 15 per cent of India's poor. Most of the poor belonging to these communities are either landless or marginal farmers.

Gender Dimension of Poverty

Although women in India were a marginalised and backward group due to socio-structural constraints imposed upon them, they have been able to improve their wellbeing in the last 30 years as a result of concerted efforts towards their upliftment (Annex 1.1). Such an improvement can be seen in terms of increased expectation of life at birth, increased age at marriage, gross enrolment ratio at all levels of education, work participation rate and organised employment and lesser gap between infant mortality rate for girls and boys. Yet, poverty in India continues to have gender dimension. With higher maternal and infant mortality rates, lower age at marriage, widespread illiteracy, higher dropout rate of girls from schools and lower work participation rates, Indian women are one of the most disadvantaged groups in the society. While in overall terms, women seem to have even better life expectancy and lesser death rates than men, more women die than men up to age 34. Infant and child mortality rates are higher for girls than boys. The worse situation is caused when birth ratio is also getting impaired due to the practice of female infanticide and the proliferation of sex-determination clinics in urban areas. Deprivation in literacy is significantly more among women. More girls dropout even at the primary stage of education than boys (Gopalan 2002: 330).

Further, the quality of employment for women leaves much to be desired. Over 90 per cent of the rural women workers are unskilled and hence, they are mainly engaged in informal/unorganised sector. Wage rates for women in agriculture have been, on an average, 30-50 per cent less than those paid to men. Besides such discrimination in wages and availability of work, women shoulder almost the entire burden of household activities and childcare responsibilities. Thus, a large proportion of women's work time is spent on such activities. This leaves little time for women to engage themselves in income generating activities (IGAs). Female casual labourers in rural India show the highest incidence of poverty of any occupational category, male or female. Women-headed households suffer from a disproportionate burden of poverty. At the same time, the structures to deliver the services of credit, technical advice, etc., do not reach them because of their gender bias. Employment of women in organised and public sectors is much lower than that for men. The presence of women in decision-making positions is nowhere near parity with men. It is found that women have been marginalised even in the plans and programmes. For example, the National Commission for Women observes that with the shrinking development expenditure on account of growing debt and interest burden on both central and state governments, the axe generally fell on social sectors including women development (Gopalan 2002: 22).

Poverty Alleviation Programmes

Indian government has been implementing employment and income generation programmes such as National Rural Employment Programme (NREP), Integrated Development Programmes (IRDP), Jawahar Rozgar Yojana (JRY) and so on since 1970s for poverty alleviation. These programmes, as discussed below, aim at employment generation, creation and/or rejuvenation of assets for the village level communities and asset building among poorer households.

In order to promote employment opportunities for the poor, the government introduced a Crash Scheme for Rural Employment (CSRE) and Drought-Prone Area Programme (DPAP) in the 1970s. The total number of workdays generated by CSRE was 178 million, while DPAP generated 37.9 million workdays of employment. However, the proportion of amount spent on these programmes to total plan outlay was generally low. Further, wages as a proportion to total expenditure was also low – especially under DPAP. Though these programmes were meant to provide employment to the "most needy", targeting was neither very specific nor very effective. Further, these programmes emphasised on developing economic infrastructure such as roads, which only indirectly contributed to the welfare of the poor. Moreover, richer segments in rural areas subverted public works programmes to serve their own interests. Overall, these programmes could not provide long-term answers to the unemployment problem among the poor.

A nation-wide National Rural Employment Programme (NREP), instituted in 1980, aimed to utilise unemployed and underemployed labour in rural areas to create productive community assets. This programme focused not only on productive assets such as irrigation infrastructure, drainage systems, and soil conservation schemes, but also on basic social services such as wells, village schools, health sub-centres, and rural housing and roads. The total amount of expenditure for NREP increased from Rs. 15 billion during 1980-85 to nearly Rs. 22 billion during the period 1985-86. However, the employment generated by the NREP was only less than 8 per cent of total unemployment in 1980. Further, NREP was not meant to provide full-time year-round employment; it merely attempted to supplement the income of the poor – "especially during the slack season".

JRY (later it was called JGSY and SGRY), which merged all the earlier employment programmes, was another major anti-poverty employment programme, which was managed and implemented by thousands of elected representatives. The primary objective of the JRY was generation of additional gainful employment for the unemployed and underemployed from among the poorer groups. The other objectives were creation of community assets for the benefit of the poor and improvement in the overall quality of life. The programme, however, faced the problems of inadequate resources, lack of people's involvement, poor implementation etc. The poor would have benefited more if their organisations had taken an active part in the selection and implementation of the projects.

Thus, two critical aspects in planning and implementation of the programmes were noted. First, lack of involvement of the people in the identification of beneficiaries and implementation of the programme. Second, the notable feature was the involvement of elected bodies in the planning and implementation of JRY. Such an involvement was considered to be a good strategy as these bodies, being closer to the people, were more suited to assess the employment needs of the poor, identify the assets most needed for the livelihoods of the community, prioritisation in the construction of assets and targeting the most needy for employment provision.

Another major anti-poverty programme was IRDP, which was initiated on a nation-wide basis in the early 1980s to increase the income generating assets of the poor directly through a mixture of subsidies and credit. IRDP, which was allocated Rs. 15 billion during the period 1980-85 and Rs. 13.49 billion during the period 1985-89, was partially successful in lifting the rural poor above the poverty line. Many irregularities in the programme were reported[6] and the space here does not permit us to list all of them and the contributing factors. But, due to non-involvement of the people in the programme, the beneficiaries selected for the programme were not always the poorest. In cases where the community was involved in the selection process, the targeting and the impact of the programme tended to be better. This suggests that if the poor represent themselves in these programmes through their own organisations, the benefits of such a massive programme like IRDP can be enormous.

These programmes, which embraced or touched upon all the problems of the poor, have started showing positive results wherever people were involved in the implementation. However, the efforts and interventions of the government are unfortunately going down the drain. It is being realised that the strategies of development ranging from individual to community development schemes failed to take benefits of development to the poorest of the poor, and also to contain and curtail vested interests who oppress and exploit the poor and appropriate the maximum benefits of the government sponsored (and managed) development programmes. It is often felt that agriculture and rural development programmes characterise goal confusion, mis-targeting and negative subsidies. The problem of leakages, pre-empting the benefits meant for the poor by the non-poor, is another major hurdle. The larger masses, weak and poor sections of society are, therefore, subjected to only theoretical empowerment. The contributing factors to this are as follows:

(i) Public institutions, which are established with a clear objective of giving support to the poor households, are not reaching them because of lack of congruence between the recipient system and delivery system.

(ii) The failure to mobilise the poor to demand services and to obtain help from the government is resulting in very little interaction with beneficiaries, and failure of delivery systems. In the absence of effective organisations, the poor could not obtain their due share from these programmes.

(iii) The poor are handicapped in responding to these signals in the absence of capabilities and pressure groups of their own.

(iv) The flow of full benefits to the poor is being undermined with the involvement of contractors, middlemen or intermediary agencies. This is happening in spite of guidelines to involve agencies capable of ensuring people's participation such as grama panchayats, village institutions, NGOs or concerned departments themselves, in implementing the community works/programmes[7].

(v) Problems of corruption, diversion and execution.

Good Governance in Poverty Alleviation Programmes

The lessons learnt from the experience of anti-poverty programmes influenced the government to re-examine the institutional arrangement for the implementation of such programmes. In the late 1990s, the government merged IRDP and other similar programmes such as Development of Women and Children in Rural Areas (DWCRA), TRYSEM, etc., and formulated a new programme called Swarnajayanti Gram Swarojgar Yojana (SGSY).

The policy makers emphasised that SGSY programme was different from all the earlier programmes. SGSY sought to enable the people to participate in the programme. This programme, being implemented by the central government all over India since 1999, aimed to promote self-employment among women and men, and enable them to cross the poverty line. The programme sought to organise the rural poor into self-help groups through the process of social mobilisation. The SHGs were expected to mobilise savings, have linkages with banks, panchayat raj institutions, and the line departments collectively decided the economic programmes to be taken up by the members. The SGSY emphasised asset building, employment and income generation among the poor; but with a difference. Community orientation of a programme, group-based approach, implementation and monitoring by grama panchayats were its chief and unique traits. The programme sought to initiate the processes such as participation, accountability and transparency for successful implementation (See, Chapter 2, for more details).

SGSY programme seems to reflect the global thinking and also the views of Indian government on 'good governance'. The term has been defined as an instrument that will help overcome the challenges of poverty and deprivation. For the Government of India, governance means the "the management of such processes that, in any society, define the environment which permits and enables the individual to raise their capability levels, on one hand, and provide opportunities to realise their potential and enlarge the set of available choices" (GoI 2002b). The policy formulators have seen a close relationship between good governance and the success of poverty alleviation efforts. The government identified the following as key factors, which adversely affected the process of implementation of rural development programmes:

- Excessive compartmentalisation of the executive into ministry/departments.
- A narrow sectoral approach to conceiving, formulating and implementing schemes.
- Prevention of mutual synergies that are inherent in most social sector programmes to benefit the plan initiatives.

Large-scale leakages and the consequent continuation of poverty and deprivation were identified as the fallout of the poor governance of the rural development programmes. The government identified the following strategies, as part of its good governance agenda, to improve the functioning of the poverty alleviation programmes.

1. Ensuring participation of the people at all stages of programme implementation.
2. Decentralisation of planning through involvement of Panchayat Raj institutions.
3. Involvement of voluntary organisations (NGOs) to supplement and complement the efforts of the government.
4. Formulation of developmental programmes in a more systematic and professional manner.
5. Right to information.
6. Empowerment of the marginalised and excluded sections of society.

Shylendra (2004) reviews the origins and development of good governance agenda. He concludes that the new good governance paradigm suggests pluralisation of the state for development. Development challenges are to be addressed collaboratively by partnerships among the State, market and civil society. The linkages and relations among different actors are to be harmonised through capacity building and co-ordination.

In the context that the SGSY programme aims to establish close linkages with decentralised institutions, and achieve the development outcomes through good governance principles of participation, transparency, accountability and linkages, the following questions become relevant. What were the processes followed in the programme implementation? Did the programme succeed in mobilising the people in the formation of SGSY groups, and in planning and implementation? What was the participation of the people in savings contribution, and borrowing from the groups? What were the linkages between the groups formed under the programme, on the one hand, and decentralised government, banks, etc., on the other? Was the right kind of synergy and harmony among multiple players generated?

Since the programme was implemented only from 1999 onwards, it may be too early to analyse the impact of the programme in terms of employment generation, asset creation and income increase. Nevertheless, one question that can be asked is: Is the programme on track in so far as achieving the objectives of enabling the poor to undertake self-employment activities for poverty reduction?

Objectives of the Study

These questions become important given that this is an all India programme with huge budgetary allocation (Chapter 2). It is in this context that the proposed study seeks to address the following objectives in relation to two districts (Betul and Chhattarpur) in Madhya Pradesh. Against the backdrop of decentralisation reforms in Madhya Pradesh, and the relative backward status of the state, it would be interesting to analyse the extent to which decentralisation and good governance have contributed to poverty alleviation through employment generation. The objectives of the study are to understand:

- what processes were followed in the formation and consolidation of the groups?

- what was the participation of people in savings contribution and borrowings from the groups?
- what were the linkages between SGSY groups, and Banks and Grama Panchayats? and
- is the programme on track in so far as achieving the objectives of enabling the poor to undertake self-employment for poverty alleviation?

The second chapter provides an overview of the policies and programmes on women development and empowerment in India. The third chapter analyses the progress of SGSY programme at the macro level. The fourth chapter provides the conceptual framework and discusses the research methodology adopted in the study. The fifth chapter analyses the participation of members in the formation and development of SGSY groups, while the sixth chapter deals with the participation of members in savings contribution and credit utilisation. The penultimate chapter deals with the linkages and synergy between SGSY groups and other actors. The final chapter provides the conclusions.

ANNEX 1.1

Selected Developmental Indicators Relating to Women

Indicators	*Total*	*Female*	*Male*	*Total*	*Female*	*Male*
Demography						
Population (in millions)	548.1	364.1 (1971)	284.0	1,027 (2001)	495.7	531.3
Decennial growth	24.6	24.9 (1971)	24.4	21.34 (1991–01)	21.79	20.93
Vital Statistics						
Sex ratio	–	930 (1971)	–	–	933 (2001)	–
Expectation of life at birth (years)	50.9 (1971)	50.2	50.5	62.9 (1996–01)	63.4	62.4
Mean age at marriage (years)	–	17.2 (1971)	22.4	–	19.4 (1995)	22.0
Health						
Birth rate	36.9 (1971)	–	–	26.1 (1999)	–	–
Death rate	15.7 (1970)	15.6	15.8	8.7 (1999)	8.3	9.0
Infant mortality rate	127 (1978)	131	123 (1999)	71.6 (1998)	72.0 (1997)	70.0 (1997)
Child mortality rate	127 (1978)	131	123	–	36.7 (1998–99)	24.9 (1998–99)
Maternal mortality	–	468 (1990)	–	–	408 (1997) 540 (1998–99)	–
Literacy and Education						
Literacy rates	16.7 (1971)	21.97	24.9	65.4 (2001)	54.2	75.9
Gross enrolment ratios						
Classes I–V	100.1	85.5	113.9	89.7	81.2	97.7
Classes VI–VIII	62.1	47.8	76.6	58.5	49.5	66.5
		(1990–91)			(1997–98)	

(Contd.)

(*Contd.*)

Indicators	*Total*	*Female*	*Male*	*Total*	*Female*	*Male*
School drop-out rates						
Classes I–V	42.6	46.0	40.1	39.6	41.3	38.2
Classes VI–VIII	60.9	65.1 (1990–91)	59.1	54.1	58.6 (1997–98)	50.7
Work and Employment						
Work participation	34.3	14.2 (1971)	52.8	37.7	22.3 (1991)	51.6
Women in the organised sector (in lakhs)	107.3	8.6 (8.0%) (1971)	155.6	283.9 (1999)	44.4 (17.4%) (1999)	234.5
Women in the public sector (in lakhs)	107.3	8.6 (8.0%) (1971)	98.7	194.3 (1996)	28.1 (14.5%) (1999)	167.9 (1996)
Women in government (in lakhs)	109.0	11.9 (11.0%) (1981)	97.1	107.7 (1999)	16.3 (15.13%) (1999)	91.4
Decision-Making						
Women in administration (actual No. in IAS, IFS & IPS)	7,102	413 (5.8%) (1987)	6,689	8,611	650 (7.6%) (1997)	7,961
Women in panchayats (in lakhs)	8.67	2.92 (33.7%) (1995) #	5.75	27.21	7.25 (26.64%) (2001)	19.96
Women in parliament (Actual No.)	768	47 (6.1%) (1989)	721	790	67 (8.4%) (1999)	723
Women in the central council of ministers (Actual No.)	40	4 (10%) (1985)	36	73	8 (10.9%) (1999)	65

Note: Figures in parenthesis indicate percentage to total, as also the year of data in respective columns wherever relevant. Although, efforts were made to keep a common 'base' and a common 'comparable' year, the same could not be kept up because of the limitations in the availability of data and other practical problems.

\# Data refer only to 7 States, viz., Haryana, Karnataka, Madhya Pradesh, Punjab, Rajasthan, Tripura and West Bengal between 1993 and 1995.

Source: Gopalan 2002.

NOTES

1. In India, the official figures on poverty are based on nutritional baseline measured in calories (food-energy method). The Planning Commission defines poverty line as per capita monthly expenditure of Rs. 49 for the rural areas and Rs. 57 for the urban areas at 1973-74 all-India prices. The poverty line corresponds to a total household per capita expenditure sufficient to provide a daily intake of 2,400 calories in rural areas and 2,100 calories in urban areas, and also basic non-food items such as clothing and transport. Individuals who fail to obtain income to meet even these basic necessities fall below the poverty line.
2. These figures have been obtained from Datt (1997).
3. These are, however, around a level considerably lower than that which prevailed in the 1970s.
4. The impact of liberalisation policies introduced in 1991 on poverty is a debated issue. It has been argued that the incidence of poverty increased in 1992 due to the introduction of macro-economic reforms. This has been, however, disputed by others (World Bank 1996: 5). While it is difficult to come to any firm conclusion regarding the impact of macro-economic policies on poverty at the macro-level, the micro-level reality suggests that the livelihood options for the poor have come under severe stress and strain after 1991. See, Joshi *et al.* 1997, and various articles in the *Economic and Political Weekly,* for more details.
5. The proportions of dalits (depressed castes) and adivasis (tribals) are relatively higher in Tamil Nadu and Andhra Pradesh. The incidence of child labour is the highest in Andhra Pradesh.
6. For details, see, GoI (1985), Rath (1990) and GoI (2001).
7. For instance, the poor in West Bengal through their organisation and participation in local civic bodies have ensured that they got their due share from all state initiated programmes. Similarly, when one NGO in Orissa could not force the contractors to pay minimum wages, it facilitated the formation of labour unions which themselves took up public works and implemented minimum wages.

2

Women Development and Empowerment: An Overview of Policies and Programmes

Introduction

SGSY is one of the largest programmes undertaken by the Department of Rural Development (DRD) in the country. Of the Rs. 42,946 crores of budget of the Department during 1999-2003, around 17 per cent was invested on SGSY programme. During the four-year period ending with 2002-03, Rs. 4,335.7 crores had been allocated to the programme. The main objective of the programme was to promote self-employment among women and men from poor households, either by providing assistance directly to the individuals (called as Swarojgaris) or through SHGs formed among them. SGSY lays emphasis on group approach, under which the poor are organised into SHGs. By the end of 2002-03, there were 1,195,023 SHGs and most of the members in the SHGs were women. The programme was initiated because of the realisation that despite efforts made by the government in the past, rural poverty continued to be significant and women development and empowerment had not been achieved to the extent it was needed. Against this background, this chapter provides an overview of the programmes initiated for women development and empowerment and a review of SGSY programme from secondary sources.

Overview of the Policies and Programmes on Women Development and Empowerment

Since independence several government policies and programmes aimed at women development and empowerment have been introduced and operationalised through the five-year plans. The policy framework and strategies for women development and empowerment were gradually evolved over time (Chart 2.1). In this regard, the Ninth Plan document states that: "In the earlier phase of developmental planning, the concept of women's development was mainly 'welfare' oriented. During the sixties, women's education received priority... During the seventies, there was a definite shift in the approach from 'welfare' to 'development' which started recognising women as participants of development. The eighties adopted a multi-disciplinary approach with a special thrust on the three core sectors of health, education and employment... The early nineties made a beginning in concentrating on training-cum-income generation programmes for women with the ultimate objective of making them economically independent and self-reliant" (GoI 2002a: 315).

Chart 2.1: Policies on Women Development and Empowerment Through Five-Year Plans

First Five Year Plan (1951-56)	Mainly welfare-oriented as far as women's issues were concerned. The Central Social Welfare Board (CSWB) undertook a number of welfare measures through the voluntary sector. The programmes for women were implemented through National Extension Service and Community Development Blocks.
Second Five Year Plan (1956-61)	Efforts were made to organise Mahila Mandals (women's groups) at the village level to ensure better implementation of welfare schemes.
Third, Fourth and other Interim Plans (1961-74)	Accorded high priority to women's education. Measures to improve maternal and child health services, and a programme ensuring supplementary food and nutrition for children and expectant mothers were introduced.

(*Contd.*)

Sixth Five Year Plan (1980-85)	Was regarded as a landmark for women's development. Women's issues, instead of treating them as welfare issues, were holistically considered in terms of consolidated development subject. The Plan adopted a multi-disciplinary approach with a three-pronged thrust on health, education and employment of women.
Seventh Five Year Plan (1985-90)	Very significant step was taken to identify and promote "beneficiary-oriented programmes" to extend direct benefits to women. The objective was to raise the economic and social status of women, and bring them into the mainstream of national development.
Eighth Five Year Plan (1992-97)	Promised to ensure that the benefits of development from different sectors did not bypass women. Special programmes were implemented to complement the general development programmes. The strategy was to maximise benefits from the latter and enhance them through the former. The flow of benefits to women in the three core sectors of education, health and employment were monitored vigilantly. Women were enabled to function as equal partners and participants in the developmental process with reservation of membership in the local bodies. This approach of the Eighth Plan marked a definite shift from 'development' to 'empowerment' of women.
Ninth Five Year Plan	Empowerment of women (especially those belonging to socially disadvantaged groups) as agents of socio-economic change and development. Promoting and developing people's participatory institutions like Panchayat Raj Institutions, co-operatives and self-help groups. Strengthening efforts to build self-reliance. Convergence of services from different sectors. Women component plans at the Central and State levels.

Such an evolution of policy framework was due to the implementation of the programmes through government and non-governmental agencies and constant review of these programmes and implementation structures. The welfare programmes in the first two five year plans were pursued through Community Development Programmes, and subsequently, Mahila Mandals were created to ensure better implementation of the programmes. The Sixth and Seventh Plans aimed at improving the employment status of women. As part of this objective, direct poverty alleviation programmes such as Integrated Rural Development Programme (IRDP)[1] and area development programmes such as National Rural Employment Programme (NREP)[2] were initiated. It was stipulated that 40 per cent of the beneficiaries under IRDP should be women.

The implementation structures were, however, not considered appropriate for the implementation of women development activities. Prior to 1975, women's development was not an exclusive portfolio. It was handled as an incidental subject under the Ministry of Social and Women's Welfare. The Central Social Welfare Board, created in 1953, was undertaking welfare schemes for women. It was in 1985 that an exclusive Department of Women and Child Development was created. It also became a political portfolio under the Ministry of Human Resource Development handled by a separate minister. The other enabling structures, such as Women Development Corporations (WDCs), were set up in 18 states to implement the new strategy of economic development of women through facilitating access to training, entrepreneurship development, credit, technical and marketing services.

The studies and evaluation reports of the area development programmes and anti-poverty programmes conclude that targeting was poor, people's involvement in planning and implementation was lacking and the impact was marginal. In cases where the target group was involved in the selection of beneficiaries under IRDP, the targeting and the impact tended to be better. This suggested that if the poor represented themselves in anti-poverty programmes through their own organisations, the benefits of programmes such as IRDP would be enormous.

The experience of some of the NGOs in women development and empowerment started to become available by the mid-1980s. Some of these NGOs (such as MYRADA) organised women in small groups (numbering 15-20) for providing awareness on their rights and entitlements, education and sought to improve their material position by enabling them to have access to credit. Women were encouraged to contribute savings to the group, and the accumulated savings fund was used to meet the consumption credit needs of the women. The studies on such initiatives came with the findings that smaller groups would help organise women, and achieve their social and economic empowerment (Fernandez 1993; Rajasekhar 1994 and 1996).

These findings resulted in important changes in approach (shift from individual beneficiary to groups of women) and strategy (organisation of women) of women development and empowerment programmes. First, the Development of Women and Children in Rural Areas (DWCRA) was started as a sub-programme of IRDP exclusively for women as it was found that women members of IRDP assisted households did not receive adequate benefits. Under this programme, the staff of DWCD at the village level formed a 15-member women group, which, after regular monthly savings of Rs.30 for six months, was eligible for an interest free loan from a local formal bank (grant in the cases of ST/SC women). As per the design, each successful repayment would make the group eligible to borrow higher amounts. The commercial banks were reported to be attracted to this programme because lending was based on the savings of women members, and larger loans were given only after the group proved itself through repayment[3]. As a result, the programme expanded rapidly[4].

The studies and evaluations on anti-poverty programmes came up with the following findings. As far as DWCRA was concerned, the group formation process became short and *ad hoc* and many groups became inactive and defunct due to "lack of orientation of the project staff, inadequate staffing, poor follow-up, target chasing and insufficient linkages" (Rajakutty 1997). Limited institutional capacity (in government as well as non-government agencies) to address the socio-economic needs of the women and target-oriented top-down approach in the programme implementation with inadequate emphasis on self-reliant thrift and credit groups also impeded women's quest for greater economic and social empowerment (World Bank 1997: 2-4). However, the initial success of DWCRA together with the fact that the groups tended to function well where NGOs were involved prompted the governments in various states to come up with similar programmes, which envisaged participation of various development actors. These programmes are called Stree-Shakthi in Karnataka and Kutumbasri in Kerala, involving banks (in financing), NGOs (in capacity building) and others in the implementation of the programmes, and building suitable linkages in this regard.

The evaluations conducted on programmes like IRDP, TRYSEM (Training for Rural Youth in Self-Employment and Management) reveal that these programmes did not yield development benefits[5] due to lack of co-ordination between the programmes and involvement of the target group. The Indian government merged all the direct anti-poverty programmes (IRDP, DWCRA, TRYSEM, etc.) into one single programme called Swarnajayanti Gram Swarojgar Yojana (SGSY) in 1999 to promote self-employment among women and men (by forming SHGs among them) and enabling them to cross the poverty line. Women constitute at least 49 per cent of the total persons assisted in the programme. SGSY sought to involve line departments, Panchayat Raj Institutions (PRIs), NGOs and CBOs in the implementation of the programme. The involvement of PRIs at all levels was considered necessary owing to the 73rd Constitutional Amendment which accorded substantial powers to PRIs and stipulated that one-third of the seats should be reserved for women.

Another important development in the 1990s was the assignment of an increasing role to NGOs[6] (Rajasekhar 2000) by the government and external donors in service provision and poverty alleviation as a part of economic reforms agenda and reducing the role of the State. One of the poverty alleviation strategies popularised by the NGOs (with the funding support from external donors) has been the delivery of micro-finance services through a group-based approach. The NGOs formed SHGs consisting of women and enabled them to undertake savings and credit activities. Although the results of these experiments were uneven across the regions, NGOs, types of groups (Rajasekhar 2002a) and their experience positively influenced the government, promotional agencies such as NABARD and SIDBI and external donors to start similar programmes on a wider scale.

Since the early 1990s, NABARD has been linking SHGs formed by NGOs, banks and government to formal banking institutions with the assistance of multi-lateral and bilateral agencies through Bank-SHG linkage programme. Under this programme, banks provide financial assistance to the SHGs for re-lending to members either directly or through the mediation of NGOs in the ratio of 1:4 of savings to credit[7]. Small Industries Development Bank also started a similar programme in 2001.

Rashtriya Mahila Kosh was set up in 1993 as part of the Department of Women and Child Development to provide credit facility to NGOs working with micro-finance groups. Between 1993 and 1999, it provided Rs. 57.62 crores to 349,752 women in micro-finance groups formed by 688 NGOs and other organisations. The recovery rate was 90 per cent (DWCD 2000).

Commercial banks, Regional Rural Banks and co-operatives also started to form SHGs (consisting mostly of women) and channel the credit under priority sector lending to the members in these groups. Although the aggregate picture on the efforts by the formal banks is not available, the indications[8] are that the banks have found micro-finance groups as viable instruments for lending to the poor and meeting the priority sector lending targets.

Not to be left behind, the World Bank and the International Fund for Agriculture and Development (IFAD) initiated a Rural Women Development and Empowerment Programme (RWDEP) with a total budget of 191.21 crores in 1999 – a five-year national project for rural women's development and empowerment. Called as Swa-Shakthi, the project was implemented by DWCD in seven States, namely, Karnataka, Gujarat, Haryana, Uttar Pradesh, Bihar,

Madhya Pradesh and Jharkhand. Under this programme, SHGs of women were formed, micro-finance activities were introduced and attempts were made to link the SHGs with banks, line departments and PRIs. The World Bank is currently planning to initiate one such programme in Tamil Nadu. Other bilateral agencies such as DRD also started similar programmes.

To sum up, the government has been formulating policies and implementing programmes for women development and empowerment. The discussion shows that there has been a shift in the policy focus from 'welfare' to 'development' and to 'empowerment' during the Five-Year Plan periods, especially after the 1970s. Further, the functions relating to women's development and empowerment were assigned to different types of local organisations, line departments, local government, NGOs and others. There was also a shift in targeting strategy from 'individual beneficiaries' to 'Self-Help Groups (SHGs) of women involved in micro-finance'.

SGSY Programme

One national programme, which incorporated the above changes in the approach and strategy in women development and empowerment, was SGSY. This section by discussing the details of the programmes with the help of policy documents of the government shows the ways in which the new approach and strategy is incorporated into the programme design.

SGSY aims to bring assisted poor households above the poverty line within a period of three years and covers 30 per cent of the poor in each block within a period of five years. It also aims to ensure that all the beneficiary households are assured of a monthly income of at least Rs. 2,000.

Functions of various development actors at different levels

The administrative structure and functions of various development actors at different levels with reference to SGSY (Chart 2.2 and Figure 2.1) have been provided below.

Chart 2.2: Functions of Local Organisations Involved in SGSY

Level	*Organisation type/functionary/ committee*	*Fina- ncing*	*Staffing*	*Provi- sioning*	*Imple- mentation*	*Capacity building*	*Coord- nation of activities*	*Monitoring and evaluation*	*Conflict resolution and accounta- bility*	*Information sharing and documen- tation*
Central	DRD	✓			✓		✓	✓		✓
State	Co-ordination Committee				✓		✓	✓		
	DRD	✓			✓	✓	✓	✓		✓
District	SGSY Committee				✓			✓	✓	
	Zilla Panchayat				✓[1]			✓		
	DRDA	✓					✓			✓
Block	SGSY Committee				✓		✓	✓		
	Taluk Panchayat							✓		
	CEO of Taluk Panchayat				✓	✓	✓			
	Banks	✓			✓			✓		
	NGOs					✓		✓		
Village	Grama Sabha								✓	
	Grama Panchayat							✓		
	SGSY Group	✓[2]		✓	✓					

Notes:

1. Approval of key activities.
2. Obtaining financial help from the banks.

State

The DRD at the state level undertakes the functions of: (a) implementing, monitoring and evaluating SGSY; (b) preparing budget estimates, releases of funds (25 per cent of the state share) and audit; (c) co-ordination and capacity building; and (d) preparation of various reports and statements. As Table 2.1 shows, the state level co-ordination committee provides guidance, seeks to co-ordinate the activities and undertakes monitoring function.

Table 2.1: Committees Constituted to Guide, Co-ordinate, Review and Monitor the Progress of SGSY

Level	*Members in the Committee*	*Functions*
National	Secretary, Ministry of Rural Development (Chairperson). Deputy Governor, Reserve Bank of India. Secretaries of departments of Agriculture and Rural Development, Expenditure, DWCD, Small Scale and Agro-related industries, Science and Technology and Ministry of Welfare. Special Secretary, Banking Division, and Ministry of Finance. Managing Director, NABARD. Adviser (Rural Development), Planning Commission. State Secretaries of Rural Development Chairman-cum-Managing Director of all Commercial Banks. Director General of CAPART Director General of NIRD	• Reviewing and ensuring effective implementation of the programme. • Reviewing linkages for support services for SGSY. • Reviewing progress of these programmes in physical, financial and qualitative terms including credit assistance. • Considering concurrent evaluation reports. • Providing a forum for a continuous dialogue with the state governments and bankers. • Reviewing the credit arrangements and recommend changes and improvements as and when necessary.

(*Contd.*)

Level	*Members in the Committee*	*Functions*
	Chairman, Indian Banks Association Joint Secretary (SGSY), Department of Rural Development (Member Secretary)	
State	Chief Secretary/Development Commissioner Secretary (Institutional Finance) Secretary (Planning) Secretary (Women's Development) Concerned Heads of Line Departments Secretary (in-charge of welfare of ST/SCs) Representatives of NABARD Representatives of RBI Representatives of Implementing Banks Representatives of GOI (Deputy Secretary) Director, SIRD Convenor, SLBC Secretary, Rural Development	• Providing leadership and guidance in planning, implementation and monitoring • Reviewing the district-wise progress of SGSY scheme • Monitoring and evaluating the programme • Reviewing the involvement of NGOs in the SGSY • Providing a forum for a dialogue between policy makers and implementers
District	District Collector/CEO DDM of NABARD LDO of RBI District Level Co-ordinators (Banks) Concerned Heads of District Level Line Departments General Manager (DIC) District KVIB Officer Project Director, DRDA NGO Representatives (2-3) Lead Bank Officer	• Reviewing the SGSY plan • Monitoring and reviewing of overall progress • Conflict resolution for inter-agency differences • Preparing items for consideration at the state level committee • Assessing the training needs and reviewing the training arrangements • Monitoring the recovery • Scrutinising the block-wise proposals in consultation with concerned experts

(*Contd.*)

Level	*Members in the Committee*	*Functions*
		• Responsible for fixing the unit cost and other techno-economic parameters
Taluk	Project Directors, DRDA Project Officer (self-employment) Branch Managers (Bank) Block Level/Sub Division Level Officers of concerned Line Departments NGO Representatives (one) Block Development Officer (Convenor)	• Selecting key activities • Selecting villages and number of beneficiaries • Distributing work among the bank branches • Monitoring the performance by different agencies • Co-ordinating activities infrastructure, credit, technology and market • Reviewing the income of the beneficiaries • Reviewing the recovery performance • Preparing monthly reports (BDO) • Preparing the pre-project report • Analysing the potential for farm activities

District

The District Rural Development Agencies (DRDAs) co-ordinate with

- its offices at taluk and below and PRIs in the implementation of the programme;
- the technical institutions for technology and training;
- the banks for planning and credit mobilisation; and
- the line departments for infrastructure, technical follow-up and marketing activities.

They also submit periodic reports on the status of SGSY to the state head of the department. The Zilla Panchayat (ZP) undertakes the functions of: (a) approving key activities, identifying the blocks with the help of district level technical group;

Fig. 2.1: Administrative Arrangement and Functions of Various Actors Involved in the Implementation of SGSY

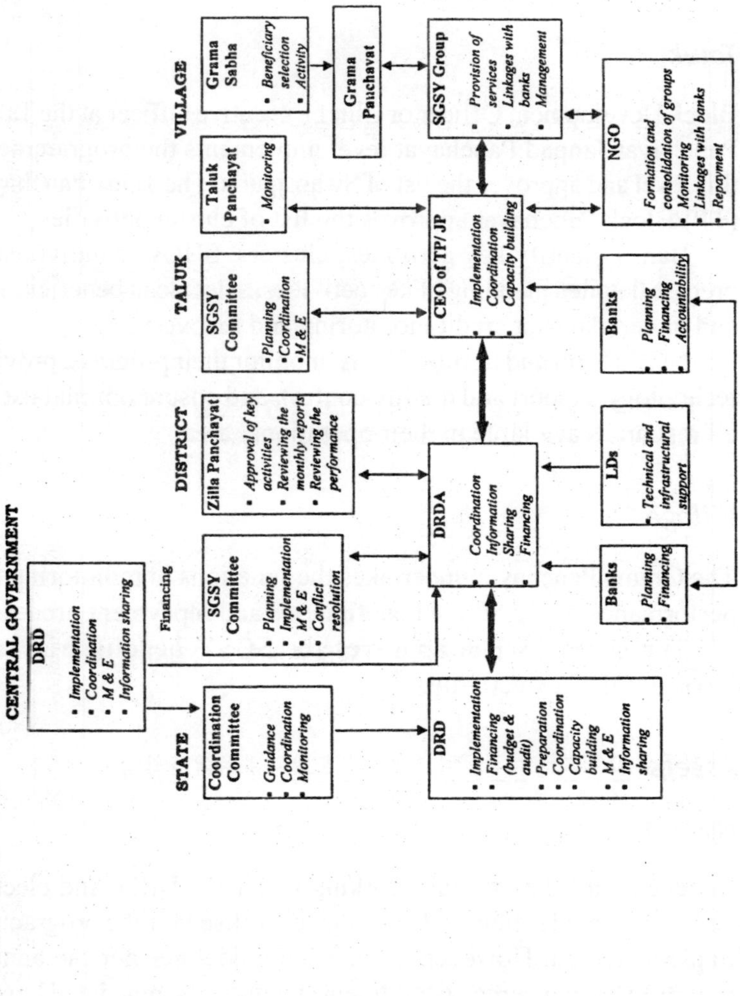

(b) reviewing of monthly reports of the block SGSY committees; and (c) reviewing the performance under SGSY in its general meetings.

SGSY committee, with the District Collector as the chairperson, and heads of relevant line departments, banks as members, undertakes the functions of co-ordination, conflict resolution and monitoring (Table 2.1).

Taluk

Block Development Officer or Chief Executive Officer at the Taluk Panchayat/Janpad Panchayat level implements the programme at this level and approves the list of Swarojgaris. The Taluk Panchayat (TP)/Block Panchayat approves the list of cluster activities.

Banks identify key activities, clusters, SHGs or individuals, prepare detailed planning of key activities, select loan beneficiaries, and undertake post credit monitoring and recovery.

NGOs form and nurture SHGs, monitor their progress, provide technology support and quality control, and ensure optimal use of all resources available in their operational area.

Village

The Grama Panchayat undertakes the functions of monitoring the performance of the SGSY beneficiaries and repayment process.

The Grama Sabha approves the SGSY beneficiaries and identifies the key activities.

Assets

Human

In general, all the officials working under the DRD, and elected and non-elected officials of PRIs can be utilised for the programme implementation. However, neither the guidelines nor the annual reports of the concerned departments mention the mandated human assets for the programme. The guidelines note that DRDA and NGOs will be involved in the implementation of the programme and also in the formation of groups and monitoring.

The personnel involved in the implementation of the project will be provided with training on formation and consolidation of SHGs, skill development, and in the gradation of SHGs. The periodicity of these training programmes is, however, not clear.

Material

The amount allocated by the Central Government to the DRD for the implementation of SGSY was Rs. 2,095 crores in 1999-2000 and Rs.1,485 crores in 2000-01. The allocation to the states was based on the incidence of poverty in the states. Additional factors such as absorption capacity (based on past trend in the utilisation of SGSY fund) and special requirement were also taken into consideration.

Each DRDA is expected to incur expenditure on training, infrastructure, revolving fund to SHG and subsidy for economic activities from the funds provided by the SGSY. The distribution of total funds by these project activities is not fixed, as SGSY is a process-oriented scheme. It is recognised that the budget under each of these heads may vary from year to year, and hence, no cap is fixed on the budget for each of these heads. It is generally expected that DRDAs should maintain a balance between the expenditure proposed under different items. However, the budget on infrastructure is not to exceed 20 per cent of the total annual allocation.

A SHG will be provided with a revolving credit fund of Rs.25,000, of which Rs.10,000 will be interest free subsidy from DRDA and Rs.15,000 will be interest bearing loan from the bank. Each SGSY group will receive material assets such as books and documents.

Organisational

- The guidelines provide for the constitution of SGSY

committees at various levels and specify the exact role of banks and promotional agencies in the implementation of the programme. These specifications are, however, in the nature of suggestions for their participation in the programme, and do not have any binding on these institutions.

- Devolution of funds to the districts will be indicated by the states and approved by the Government of India. The funds will be directly released to DRDAs.
- All the assets (such as livestock) acquired by the beneficiaries as part of programme benefits will have to be insured. The General Insurance Corporation has agreed to provide insurance cover as per the agreement signed between the insurance corporation and the state government.
- In order to promote credit discipline among Swarojgaris and also to bring about a sense of accountability among the community, the following incentive and disincentive system has been introduced:
  - (a) Prompt repayment will entitle each Swarojgari to a waiver of 0.5 per cent of processing-cum-monitoring fee.
  - (b) Grama and block panchayats have to ensure a minimum of 80 per cent of recovery in grama panchayat and block panchayat areas. Those grama and block panchayats that do not fulfil the required recovery performance will not be eligible for any allocation under SGSY in the subsequent year.
- The SHGs, by and large, are informal groups; but, they can be registered if required under the Societies Act and Co-operatives Act. SHGs can also be federated at cluster, taluk or district levels depending on the number of SHGs and spatial distribution.
- It is stipulated that the DRDAs should put concerted efforts to strengthen and consolidate SHGs formed by the earlier programmes such as DWCRA, NGO programmes, banks, Swa-Shakthi, Swayam-Sidda, etc., and then take steps to form new groups (GoI 1999: 11).

Processes

Participation

The beneficiaries under the SGSY can be either individuals or groups. SGSY lays emphasis on the group approach, under which the poor are organised into SHGs. In either case, the list of households below the poverty line, duly approved by the Grama Sabha will form the basis for the identification of households (GoI 1999: 8). However, if it is absolutely required, 30 per cent of the members can be selected from households marginally above the poverty line. The proportion of SHGs consisting of women to total groups should be 50 per cent.

At the beginning of each year, the Swarojgaris, having potential to undertake economic activities, are identified in each habitation by a three-member committee including the Sarpanch. The list of Swarojgaris who are sanctioned the loan by the banks are placed before the Grama Sabha.

The development of a SHG has been envisaged to be in four phases. The group formation phase involves forming 10-20 member affinity groups enabling them to prepare a code of conduct and hold meetings independently. The group stabilisation phase coveres regular savings and borrowings from the savings fund. The micro-credit phase involves obtaining financial support from the banks under NABARD Bank-SHG linkage programme. The phase of micro-enterprise development emphasises on skill development and upgradation, activity development and marketing support.

The approach to be followed in the formation and development of SHGs should be process-oriented as against the target-oriented one (GoI 1999: 11).

SGSY gives importance to the cluster approach. DRDA identifies four to five key activities, which will be approved by the Taluk/Janpad Panchayats at the Taluk level and Zilla Panchayat/ DRDAs at the district level. The total funds to be allocated to cluster activities are 75 per cent of the total budget. The banks and other financial institutions are closely associated and involved in preparing project reports for each key activity so as to avoid delays in sanctioning loans and to ensure adequacy of financing.

SGSY recognises that group formation and development are not spontaneous, and there is need for facilitation by committed and dedicated staff or organisations. Hence, NGOs, CBOs, network of community organisers and team of dedicated staff can facilitate the process-oriented implementation of the programme. DRDAs select such organisations based on the criteria provided in the guidelines.

An elaborate gradation process is to be adopted to assess the status of SGSY groups, arrive at the type of capacity building inputs to be provided and enable the groups to have linkages with the banks (GoI 1999: 12-13). The guidelines emphasise the participatory approach to gradation, which is to be done at several phases of the group's growth, in which group members, promoting agency, government officials and banks are involved. After the first grading (when the group completes six months of the period), the group will be provided with a revolving credit fund of Rs.25,000. The group will be subjected to second gradation process six months after receiving the revolving fund to ascertain whether the group has been functioning effectively and is capable of taking up an economic activity through higher levels of investment.

Accountability

In order to ensure that Swarojgaris cross the poverty line, regular follow up of the member households by DRDA/block officials and bankers (including annual verification of assets) has been suggested. Such a follow up aims to ensure proper management of assets, generation of projected income and work towards the removal of any difficulties that the Swarojgaris may be facing. A mechanism in this regard is *Vikas Pathrika,* a copy of which is issued to each Swarojgari and another is kept at the block head-quarters, for obtaining regular update on the health of a project undertaken by a Swarojgari.

Monthly progress reports should be sent from block to district to state and to central government. The progress report should reach the central government by the 20th of every month.

State level officers dealing with SGSY shall visit the districts regularly to ascertain whether the programme implementation is in accordance with the prescribed procedures and specifications. Likewise, officials at the district and block levels must closely monitor the programme. The number of Swarojgaris to be visited in each month is specified for the officers at the district and below.

The provision that all reports are to be reviewed by GP, TP and ZP implies that the implementing machinery is accountable to the PRIs.

Transparency

- The list of households selected under the BPL category, and included in the SGSY programme is to be placed before the Grama Sabha.
- The beneficiaries selected for providing financial assistance are also to be placed before the Grama Sabha.
- The key activities identified by the district and block SGSY committees are to be placed before the panchayat samithis, so that members of the panchayat samithis are aware of selection and also the members that underline the selection of villages.
- The panchayat samithi reviews the reports sent by the block SGSY committee and also recovery performance.
- The Zilla Panchayat also reviews the performance under SGSY in its general meetings.

Conclusions

The good governance paradigm gained prominence in the context of mixed results that we obtained in reducing poverty and deprivation. Although the proportion of population living below the poverty line declined, such a decline has not been uniform across the regions and social groups. In particular, women seem to be suffering from disproportionate burden of poverty. Further, the problem of poverty seems to have entered into a new dynamic and complex process. This calls for a specific set of policies to prevent the non-poor falling into poverty in addition to those aimed at poverty alleviation.

Poverty in India has a strong gender dimension. In order to develop and empower women, the government has been formulating policies and programmes, which have been operationalised through Five-Year Plans since independence. A review of the policies and programmes is undertaken during and at the end of each plan period while preparing plan documents. Such a constant review, based on evaluation and studies conducted on government-initiated women development and empowerment programmes, and the successful 'programmes' of civil society organisations within and outside the country, together with political mobilisation of women, have resulted in the following changes:

- A shift in policy focus from 'welfare' to 'development' and to 'empowerment' during the five-year plan periods, especially after the 1970s.
- Assignment of functions relating to women's development and empowerment to different types of local organisations, line departments, local government, NGOs and others.
- Mandatory representation of women in the decentralised government at the district and below.
- Formation of grassroots level women's organisations for their development and empowerment.
- A shift in targeting strategy from 'individual beneficiaries' to 'Self-Help Groups (SHGs) of women involved in micro-finance'.
- A shift in strategy from issuing loans to individual beneficiaries to using micro-finance as an instrument for development and empowerment of women organised in SHGs.

All these indicate that good governance principles have been sought to be applied to women development and empowerment programme. SGSY represents one such programme. This chapter has provided a detailed discussion on functions assigned to several organisations, the resources that have been provided and processes that have to be adopted in the SGSY programme. Let us now discuss the progress of the SGSY programme at the national level as well as in Madhya Pradesh.

NOTES

1. IRDP was initiated on a nation-wide basis in the late 1980s to increase the income generating assets of the poor directly through a mixture of subsidies and credit. The programme was allocated Rs.15 billion during the period 1985-89.
2. Instituted in 1980, this nation-wide programme aimed to utilise unemployed and under-employed labour in rural areas to create productive community assets such as irrigation infrastructure, drainage systems, and soil conservation schemes and also basic services such as wells, village schools, health sub-centres, rural housing and roads. The total amount of expenditure was Rs.15 billion during 1980-85 and Rs.22 billion during 1985-86.
3. In practice, this was not widespread as the quality of the groups determined the equal distribution and proper utilisation of the loan amount.
4. The number of groups increased from 28,031 (with 4.69 lakh members) by the end of 1989-90 to 86,774 (with 14.96 lakh members) by November 1994. During this period, the achievement exceeded the target by more than 100 per cent (Rajakutty 1997:91).
5. Sustainable poverty alleviation did not take place (Rath 1985 and Rajasekhar and Vyasulu 1990) due to lack of congruence between delivery and recipient systems, and lack of co-ordination between various government departments implementing the anti-poverty programmes leading to overlapping and duplication.
6. The political space now available for the NGOs (Webster and Engberg-Pedersen 2002) is the result of the growth of NGO sector, which is, to a large extent, supported by external donors. The gradual

recognition by the state of the possibilities and potential of involving the NGO sector in anti-poverty programmes has enhanced the legitimacy of NGOs. Interface with the state and government agencies at different levels (Rajasekhar and Reddy 1997; Reddy and Rajasekhar 1996) has been found very useful in advocating policy changes in favour of the poor, although it is not a smooth process.

7. The programme covers 458,666 SHGs (90 per cent of which are exclusively for women) in 412 districts in 27 states and union territories. In all, 7.9 million poor households gained access to formal banking system through this programme.
8. For instance, the Cauvery Grameen Bank (CGB) with capacity inputs from MYRADA promoted 398 SHGs (with over 6,000 members) by June 2000. Of these groups, 184 were linked to banks, and the total amount of credit disbursed was Rs. 40.42 lakhs. The total amount of savings contributed by these groups was Rs. 45.67 lakhs (CGB 2000: 15).

3

Progress of SGSY Programme: Analysis at the Macro Level

Introduction

SGSY is one of the largest programmes undertaken by the Department of Rural Development in all the Indian States and Union territories for the promotion of self-employment among women and men from poor households, either by providing assistance directly to the individuals (called Swarojgaris) or through SHGs formed among them. The programme was initiated because of the realisation that despite the government efforts in the past, rural poverty continue to be significant. Conceived as a holistic programme, SGSY combined the earlier anti-poverty programmes from April 1999, and covered all aspects of self-employment like mobilisation of the poor into SHGs, training, credit, technology, infrastructure and marketing. As noted earlier, SGSY aims to raise assisted poor households above the poverty line within three years and covers 30 per cent of the poor in each block within five years. It also aims to ensure that all the beneficiary households are assured of a monthly income of at least Rs. 2,000. In the first year, individual households are directly provided with assistance. Subsequently, the SHGs are formed among both women and men for the purpose of promoting self-employment opportunities among them.

What has been the progress of the programme in terms of funds allocation and utilisation, credit mobilisation by Swarojgaris and provision of subsidy to them and the growth in the number of SHGs formed and in the number of SHG members? What has been the progress in the number of swarojgaris assisted under the programme? How many groups accessed the credit from external agencies such as banks? This chapter seeks to provide answers based on the secondary data collected at the all India level as well as for the state of Madhya Pradesh. The data used in this paper were collected from the Ministry of Rural Development, New Delhi, and pertains to the five-year period of 1999-2000 to 2003-04 (henceforth, five-year period). Though data are available for a few months in 2004-05, we have confined our analysis to this five-year period as the figures for a few months in the latest year disturb the overall trends.

Financial Performance

The provision of sufficient financial resources and their utilisation are important for the success of a programme such as SGSY, which is meant to be process-oriented. Further, the programme seeks to incorporate good governance principles of participation, transparency and accountability. All this means that there needs to be sufficient and timely availability of financial resources to the programme. In order to assess the financial performance of the programme, this section looks at allocations and utilisation, purpose-wise distribution of the financial resources, availability of credit facility to swarojgaris.

Allocations and utilisation

SGSY, being a centrally sponsored programme, is financed by both central and state governments in the ratio of 75:25. The procedure adopted in the allocation of funds to states, districts and blocks has been briefly explained below. The central government allocates the financial resources to the states on the basis of incidence of poverty in a particular state. Other parameters that come into the reckoning are absorption capacity of a state and special requirements, if any. The former will be arrived at after looking at the progress made in the utilisation of allocated funds. After the allocation of the financial resources to each of the states by the central government, the funds will be directly released to the District Rural Development Agency (DRDA). The governing body of the DRDA decides the allocation of funds to different taluks. This will be done on the basis of incidence of poverty and other local factors.

Table 3.1 shows that the total allocation to the programme in the country as a whole was Rs. 4,335.7 crores during the five-year period. The allocation, which was Rs.1,472 crores in the first year, however, declined in the subsequent years, and reached the lowest figure of Rs.756 crores in 2002-03. An important reason for the dwindling allocation was growing or high opening balance in the first three years of the programme. In the second year, the amount of the opening balance was over 50 per cent of the total amount allocated. This indicates that the programme was facing teething problems in so far as the utilisation of the allocated amounts was concerned.

Table 3.1: Allocation and Release of Funds (Rs. in crores) to SGSY Programme (1999-2000 to 2003-2004)

Items	*Years*					
	1999-2000	*2000-01*	*2001-02*	*2002-03*	*2003-04*	*All years*
1. Total allocation	1,472	1,333	775	756	1,066	5,402
2. Misc. receipt	54	91	81	77	89	392
3. Opening balance as on 1st April	777	855	662	416	287	2,996
4. Central allocation	1,105	1,000	582	568	800	4,054
5. Central releases	870	462	401	505	645	2,882
6. Proportion of 5 to 4	78.69	46.21	68.98	88.85	80.64	68.75
7. State allocation	367	333	193	188	266	1,347
8. State releases	261	201	156	181	192	992
9. Proportion of 8 to 7	71.18	60.38	80.87	96.11	72.30	73.93

Source: Annual Report 2003-04, Ministry of Rural Development, Govt. of India.

Gradually, there was a decline in the amount of opening balance. This prompted setting up the overall allocation to Rs.1,066 crores in 2003-04. The amount allocated to SGSY further increased to Rs.1,333 crores in 2004-05 as the opening balance was the lowest at Rs.192 crores in this year. The discussion, thus, suggests that SGSY programme gradually acquired the capacity to spend the amounts allocated under the programme. Even then, the amount allocated had not reached the level of 1999-2000 in any of the subsequent years.

The releases by the central and state governments are governed by the extent to which the DRDAs have managed to spend the amounts allocated to them. This makes it necessary to analyse the proportion of releases to total allocations to obtain some clues on the capacity and performance of rural development agencies in the programme. The percentage of central releases to total allocations was 79 per cent in 1999-2000. This percentage declined to 46 in 2000-01 and 69 in 2001-02 (Table 3.1). Subsequently, the proportion of releases increased. In contrast, the proportion of releases from state governments to total state allocations was higher than that by the central government in three out of five years. An important point to note is that the proportion of releases to allocation was never cent per cent in the case of both state and central governments. This suggests the capacity related problems among rural development agencies in the utilisation of allocated amount, and/or problems in the disbursal of amounts allocated to them.

A similar picture emerges in Madhya Pradesh State and the selected districts. Of the total allocated amount of Rs.80.11 crores for 2003-04, the total funds available with the programme at the state level was only Rs.47.69 crores. The proportion of available funds was somewhat better in Betul district (Annex 3.1).

Utilisation of financial resources

An examination of trends in the utilisation of allocated and available funds would provide clues on why releases were not equal to allocations in almost all the years. Table 3.2 shows gradual increase in the proportion of utilised funds to total allocated funds.

In fact, the amount utilised was more than the allocation during 2001-02 to 2002-03. This became possible due to large amount of opening balance in these years. Because of this reason, it becomes necessary to examine the utilisation of available funds.

The percentage of utilised funds to the total available funds was less than 50 per cent in 1999-2000. This gradually increased to 86.01 per cent by 2003-04. This again shows the growing capacity of the programme to utilise the finances available. Yet, the utilisation of available funds was not close to 100 per cent. This calls for an examination of purpose-wise utilisation of available funds.

Each DRDA is expected to incur expenditure on training, infrastructure and subsidy for economic activities as well as towards revolving fund from the funds available for SGSY programme. Since SGSY is meant to be process-oriented programme and the budget under each of these heads is likely to vary every year, no cap is fixed on budget for these heads. The expectation is, however, that DRDAs should maintain a balance between expenditure proposed under different items. Further, the expenditure on infrastructure should not exceed 20 per cent of the total annual allocation. Against this background, let us now examine the trends in expenditure on these heads.

Provision of subsidy

As noted earlier, a SHG will be provided with a revolving fund of Rs.25,000 after it passes through grade I. Of the total revolving fund, Rs.10,000 will be interest free subsidy from DRDA.

In addition, when the group passes grade II and is ready to undertake the income generating activity, it is entitled to another round of subsidy. Subsidy under SGSY will be uniform at 30 per cent of the project cost (Rs. 25,000) subject to a maximum of Rs. 7,500. In respect of SC/STs, however, this will be 50 per cent. There will be no monetary limit on subsidy for irrigation projects. For Groups of Swarojgaris belonging to BPL households, the subsidy will be at 50 per cent of the cost of the scheme, subject to a ceiling of Rs. 1.25 lakhs. The number of borrowers in a group may vary from 10 to 20. In the case of groups for minor irrigation and among the disabled, the number can be as low as five. The list of BPL households identified through BPL census, duly approved by the Grama Sabha, will form the basis for identification of the households for SGSY assistance. A maximum of 70 per cent of the total funds allotted to each DRDA can be utilised as subsidy under group ventures with no such ceiling on the quantum of credit[1].

Table 3.2 reveals that the programme has done very well in utilising the budget allocated for subsidy. Beginning with 36.79 per cent in 1999-2000, the proportion of amount provided as subsidy to total allocated amount for this head gradually increased and reached 148 per cent in 2003-04. The same emerges if one looks at the district-wise picture in Madhya Pradesh. In the State as a whole, the subsidy as a proportion of the total expenditure was 65.61 per cent. This was as much as 76 per cent in Betul and 68.11 per cent in Chhattarpur (Annex 3.1).

Table 3.2: Utilisation of Allocated and Available Funds (1999-2000 to 2003-2004)

Items	*Years*					
	1999-2000	*2000-01*	*2001-02*	*2002-03*	*2003-04*	*All years*
1. Total allocation (Rs. in crores)	1,472	1,333	775	756	1,066	5,402
2. Total funds available (Rs. in crores)	1,961	1,608	1,300	1,178	1,214	7,261
3. Total funds utilised (Rs. in crores)	960	1,118	970	921	1,044	5,013
4. Proportion of 3 to 1	65.19	83.9	125.28	121.78	97.97	115.63
5. Proportion of 3 to 2	48.92	69.52	74.67	78.18	86.01	69.04
6. %age of utilisation on subsidy	36.79	52.67	86.16	80.1	148.35	51.14
7. %age utilisation on infrastructure	14.45	20.51	19.79	18.01	4.83	14.55
8. %age utilisation on training/skill	3.03	3.62	6.23	5.44	2.36	3.66

Source: *Annual Report 2003-04,* Ministry of Rural Development, Govt. of India.

Infrastructure development

SGSY programme aims to enhance self-employment potential among swarojgaris by way of promoting economic activities among them. Such a promotion not only requires financial support but also infrastructure in rural areas. For this, SGSY is proposed to follow a cluster approach in the programme implementation in villages. A cluster is not merely a geographic agglomeration of villages but units where backward and forward linkages can be effectively established. The programme envisages the selection of villages on the basis of facilitating factors such as setting up of infrastructure, raw material distribution, technology transfer and quality control (GoI 2004). SGSY, thus, recognises that proper infrastructure is crucial for the success of individual income generating activities, and seeks to ensure that the infrastructure needed for the identified activities is fully provided. Infrastructure includes production, processing, quality testing, storage and marketing.

The trends in the proportion of the amount utilised for infrastructure (Table 3.2) suggest that there was a hiatus between the vision and actual practice. The proportions of budgeted amount spent on infrastructure were between 4.83 and 20.51 during the five-year period. A noteworthy point is that while the proportion of budgeted amount spent on infrastructure was low, that on the provision on subsidy was not only high but also increased rapidly. This leads to a suggestion that economic activities under SGSY programme were supported without creating the necessary infrastructure in the villages. The same holds good in the case of the selected state and districts as well. While the expenditure on infrastructure provision was as low as 13.7 per cent in Madhya Pradesh, it was a mere 7 per cent in Betul and 0.5 per cent in Chhattarpur (Annex 3.1).

Expenditure on training

SGSY is often described as a holistic programme. The promotion of individual income generating activities for ensuring self-employment among the poor, especially women, is sought to be done by organising them into SHGs, building their capacity, planning of activity clusters, infrastructure support and establishing linkages for technology transfer, credit provision and marketing. The working group of the Planning Commission on rural poverty alleviation programmes for the 10th Five-Year Plan notes that social mobilisation of the poor in rural areas is an important feature of SGSY programme. It also states that social mobilisation is a basic prerequisite before assistance to take up economic activities is provided. According to the working group, the programme departs from the earlier ones in the emphasis on SHG approach for the social mobilisation of the poor. The report by the working group also makes it clear that there should not be over-emphasis on quicker results because a target-oriented approach will come in the way of social mobilisation and leads to the danger of meeting the same fate that was met by the earlier programmes (GoI 2001). In order to achieve the objective of social mobilisation, the SGSY programme seeks to entrust the responsibility of formation of groups to NGOs. Where this is not possible, the staff involved in the formation should be provided with adequate training in social mobilisation.

The two important activities of SGSY programme, namely, consolidation of groups and the promotion of individual economic activities among swarojgaris also necessitate training and skill upgradation. It is to be noted that members of SHGs need training in the organisation of meetings, preparation of rules and regulations for the group, preparation of accounts, etc. All these activities would help SGSY groups to become strong and self-sustaining in the long run. Realising the importance of these activities, SGSY programme made a provision for providing training in the allocation of resources.

Training is also needed for the promotion of economic activities. Under the cluster approach, the emphasis is on the selection of a few activities instead of providing finance to diverse activities. Cluster approach also aims at giving equal attention to different aspects of income generating activities so that swarojgaris would be able to gain sustainable income from their investment. The vision is that the choice of activity should be based on local resources, the attitude and skill of the people. The block SGSY committee is expected to build upon the traditional knowledge of the poor in the selection of suitable income generating activities. The committee would identify 8-10 activities and prioritise them. The district committee would prepare the final list of activities after vetting them. The focus would, therefore, be on 4-5 key activities in a block under the cluster approach. The line departments are expected to provide required services to swarojgaris. Where knowledge transfer is involved, the SGSY committee should facilitate such a transfer through training and skill upgradation.

From the above, it is clear that training should precede the activity of promoting income generating activities through the provision of credit support. Table 3.2, however, shows that the proportion of budgeted amount spent on training ranged from as low as 2.36 per cent to 6.23 per cent. This suggests that the support for economic activities has been provided without providing the necessary training to swarojgaris.

The proportion of expenditure on training and capacity building was 6.44 per cent in Madhya Pradesh during 2003-04. Thus, the level of expenditure on training in the State was higher than the national figure. The figures for the selected districts were, however, lower than the state figure. The proportion of expenditure on training and capacity building was 4.02 per cent in Betul, while it was only 3.88 per cent in Chhattarpur during 2003-04 (Annex 3.1).

Investment by Swarojgaris

SHG approach followed under SGSY programme seeks to build upon the savings contributed by swarojgaris and credit mobilised from banks under NABARD's bank-SHG linkage programme. As explained in Chapter 2, each SHG is expected to pass through two grades. If a SHG passes through grade I, it will obtain a revolving fund of Rs.25,000. When grade II is complete, it can access the credit from banks. The criteria adopted in the gradation include indicators on the extent to which the group is able to adopt participatory processes (meetings, election of representatives, etc.), the capacity of the group in maintaining their own accounts, progress in savings mobilisation, availing of credit and repayment. The criteria included, thus, seek to ensure that a group passes the two grades only when it is strong in self-management and credit discipline. Since only the groups which pass through the grades are eligible to obtain credit, the trends in credit mobilised by swarojgaris provide indication on the success of the programme in forming strong SHGs, inculcation of savings habit and incorporating credit discipline.

Table 3.3 provides trends in credit mobilised by swarojgaris during the five-year period. Of the Rs. 3,205 crores of credit target fixed for 1999-2000, the achievement was Rs.1,056 crores (33 per cent). In the subsequent two years, the credit targets were roughly the same. The performance of the programme in terms of meeting the target had not substantially improved. This perhaps influenced the programme implementers to reduce the total credit target to Rs. 2,525 crores in 2002-03 and to Rs. 2,129 crores in 2003-04. The total credit mobilised from the banks declined to Rs.1,184 crores in 2002-03. Even then the proportion of credit mobilised to the total target showed an increase because of reduction in the target. Thus, the programme had not met the targets that it had set for itself in so far as credit mobilisation for swarojgaris.

There were variations across the states in so far as the credit mobilised to total target. The percentage of credit mobilised to the target was more than 100 per cent in Madhya Pradesh while it was as low as 25.31 per cent in West Bengal. In general terms, the percentage of credit mobilised to the credit target was more than 75 per cent in 8 out of 20 major states, between 50 and 75 per cent in nine states and less than 50 per cent in the remaining three states (Table 3.4). It is to be noted that commercial banks accounted for nearly 64 per cent of the total credit mobilised in the country. Except in Maharashtra and Tamil Nadu states, the co-operative banks accounted for insignificant proportion of the credit

Table 3.3: Trends in Credit Mobilised by Swarojgaris (1999-2000 to 2003-04)

Items	*Years*					
	1999-2000	*2000-01*	*2001-02*	*2002-03*	*2003-04*	*All years*
1. Total credit target (Rs. in crores)	3,205	3,205	3,201	2,525	2,129	14,265
2. Total credit mobilised (Rs. in crores)	1,056	1,459	1,330	1,184	1,301	6,331
3. Proportion of 2 to 1	32.96	45.54	41.54	46.9	61.11	45.61
4. Credit disbursed to SHGs (Rs. in crores)	187	257	318	459	708	1,929
5. Proportion of 4 to 1	5.84	8.01	9.95	18.18	33.24	15.04
6. Credit disbursed to individual Swarojgaris (Rs. in crores)	869	1,203	1,011	725	593	4,402
7. Proportion of 6 to 1	27.12	37.53	31.6	28.72	27.87	30.56

Source: Annual Report 2003-04, Ministry of Rural Development, Govt. of India.

mobilised. Regional Rural Banks also provided significant proportion of the total credit (Table 3.4).

There were also variations in percentage credit mobilised to total target across districts in Madhya Pradesh during 2003-04. The percentage achievement was 100 per cent in Betul, while it was only 34.82 per cent in Chhattarpur (Annex 3.2).

The credit disbursed to individual swarojgaris was initially high as compared to that disbursed to SHGs. Although the proportion of credit disbursed to SHG to total credit mobilised increased gradually to 33.24 per cent by 2003-04, the average for the five-year period was only 15.04 per cent (Table 3.3).

Correspondingly, the total subsidy disbursed to SGSY beneficiaries also increased with fluctuations (Table 3.5). Beginning with Rs.542 crores in 1999-2000, the total subsidy increased to Rs.713 crores by 2003-04. In the first four years of the programme, the proportion of subsidy disbursed to individual

Table 3.4: Credit Disbursed (Rs. in lakhs) by the Banks to Swarojgaris in Major States of India During 2003-04

States	*Total Credit Target*	*Credit disbursed by*					
		Commercial Banks	*Co-operative Banks*	*Regional Rural Banks*	*Others*	*Total*	*% Credit disbursed to credit target*
Andhra Pradesh	11,620	5,917	220	2,766	110	9,013	77.57
Assam	14,160	3,032	307	1,531	372	5,242	37.02
Bihar	27,393	13,498	60	7,744	0	21,302	77.77
Chhattisgarh	6,034	2,089	487	1,264	66	3,907	64.76
Gujarat	4,373	2,078	485	663	58	3,284	75.09
Haryana	3,537	1,563	310	598		2,471	69.87
Himachal Pradesh	2,245	1,074	388	374	2	1,837	81.83
Jammu & Kashmir	3,113	971	525	150	34	1,680	53.95
Jharkhand	9,345	4,144	0	1,555	36	5,735	61.38
Karnataka	8,604	3,590	979	1,703	233	6,505	75.6
Kerala	3,891	1,760	599	158	0	2,517	64.68
Madhya Pradesh	13,271	9,360	820	2,662	555	13,398	100.96
Maharashtra	16,513	7,177	1,749	1,011	27	9,963	60.34
Orissa	11,122	4,539	500	2,747	3	7,790	70.04
Punjab	1,539	1,235	14	176	1	1,426	92.64
Rajasthan	8,208	4,799	661	2,425	80	7,965	97.05
Tamil Nadu	7,332	2,907	1,051	155	19	4,131	56.35
Uttar Pradesh	37,055	11,372	865	10,638	386	23,261	62.77
Uttaranchal	3,436	959	291	300	0	1,549	45.09
West Bengal	13,779	2,143	41	1,304	0	3,488	25.31
India	212,933	92,259	10,559	40,343	2,084	145,244	**68.21**

Source: *Annual Report 2003-04*, Ministry of Rural Development, Govt. of India.

swarojgaris to the total subsidy was more than 50 per cent. In fact, it was as much as 77 per cent in the first year. In contrast, the proportion of subsidy disbursed to SHG members to total was about 23 per cent in the first two years of the programme and increased to about 62 per cent by 2003-04. Table 3.5, thus, suggests that the programme was focusing on individual swarojgaris. And the activities such as social mobilisation were not yielding very good results in the first four years of the programme. This is borne out by the lower proportion of subsidy disbursed to SHG members.

Table 3.5: Trends in Subsidy Disbursed to Individual Swarojgaris and SHG Members (1999-2000 to 2003-2004)

Items	*Years*					
	1999-2000	*2000-01*	*2001-02*	*2002-03*	*2003-04*	*All years*
1. Total subsidy disbursed (Rs. in crores)	542	702	666	606	713	3,228
2. Subsidy disbursed to SHGs (Rs. in crores)	125	168	210	283	444	1,229
3. Proportion of 2 to 1	22.99	23.92	31.54	46.63	62.34	37.48
4. Subsidy disbursed to individual Swarojgaris (Rs. in crores)	417	534	456	323	269	1,999
5. Proportion of 4 to 1	76.94	76.07	68.45	53.36	37.66	62.50

Source: Annual Report 2003-04, Ministry of Rural Development, Govt. of India.

Credit mobilised from banks together with subsidy provided by the programme constitute the total investment, which increased from Rs.1,598 crores in 1999-2000 to Rs.2,014 crores by 2003-04 (Table 3.6). Although the total investment was fluctuating during the five-year period, per capita investment remained the same around Rs.22,000 during the period 2001-02 to 2003-04. The per capita investment was substantially high in Madhya Pradesh as well as in the selected districts (Annex 3.2).

An examination of credit subsidy ratio becomes important to gauge the extent to which the beneficiaries were depending on subsidies. The ratio, which was 1.95 in 1999-2000, increased to 2.08 in 2000-01 and 2.00 in 2001-02. Such an increase suggests the growing importance of subsidies in the programme. The ratio, however, declined in the last two years of the programme and thereby suggesting the emphasis on credit mobilisation in the programme probably due to the growing importance of SHGs in credit mobilisation and disbursement of subsidy.

Table 3.6: Per Capita Investment and Credit-Subsidy Ratio (1999-2000 to 2003-2004)

Items	*Years*					
	1999-2000	*2000-01*	*2001-02*	*2002-03*	*2003-04*	*All years*
1. Total investment (Rs. in crores)	1,598	2,161	1,995	1,790	2,014	9,558
2. Per capita investment (Rs. in crores)	17,113	21,481	21,284	21,666	22,469	104,013
3. Credit Subsidy Ratio	1.95	2.08	2.00	1.95	1.83	1.96

Source: *Annual Report 2003-04*, Ministry of Rural Development, Govt. of India.

To conclude, an analysis of allocations and utilisation of funds for SGSY programme shows that the allocations had, in general, declined. The proportion of releases by the central and state governments was nowhere close to 100 per cent during the entire five-year period. This suggests the capacity related problems among rural development agencies in the utilisation of allocated amounts and/or problems in the disbursal of allocated amounts.

The amount utilised by the programme was generally higher than the allocated amount during the five-year period largely due to high opening balance amount. The proportion of funds utilised to the available funds for the programme generally improved; but, never close to 100 per cent. The shortfall in the expenditure was mainly on account of less expenditure on infrastructure development and skill related training. Although the programme envisaged that the promotion of income generating activities among swarojgaris to be followed by the development of infrastructure in the village where the beneficiaries were located and provision of training to them, the budget utilisation shows that this was not the case. While the programme did well in releasing the subsidy for swarojgaris, the expenditure on skill development and infrastructure provision lagged behind. An obvious implication of this is that the credit for income generating activities to swarojgaris was provided without the necessary infrastructure and social mobilisation of the poor.

The gradation criteria adopted in the programme seek to ensure that a group passes the grades I and II only when it is strong in self-management and credit discipline. Since only the groups which pass through the grades are eligible to obtain credit, the trends in credit mobilised by swarojgaris provide an indication on whether the programme succeeded in forming strong SHGs, inculcation of savings habit and incorporating credit discipline. The data, however, show that the proportion of achievement to the target fixed on credit mobilisation ranged between 33 per cent in 1999-2000 to 61.11 per cent in 2003-04. Further, an improvement in the achievement was more because of reduction in the target rather than credit mobilised by swarojgaris. The proportion of subsidy disbursed to SHGs was lower than that provided to individual swarojgaris. This leads to two suggestions. First, since the subsidy disbursed was in proportion to the credit mobilised by swarojgaris, the implication is that the programme was focussing on individual swarojgaris. Second, the activities such as social mobilisation were not yielding very good results.

Physical Progress

Having discussed the financial progress of SGSY programme, let us analyse the trends in the physical progress of the programme in this section. The aspects covered in the section are: progress in the formation and gradation of SGSY groups; number of swarojgaris assisted; and coverage of swarojgaris belonging to disadvantaged and vulnerable groups.

Progress in the formation of SGSY groups

The total number of SHGs formed was nearly 3 lakhs in 1999-2000. Gradually, the number of groups formed under the programme in a year increased from 5.16 lakhs in 2000-01 to 17.41 lakhs in 2003-04. At the end of 2003-04, there were 48.48 lakh SGSY groups in the country as a whole. This was no doubt a spectacular achievement under the programme.

In Madhya Pradesh, there were 232,235 SHGs formed under SGSY programme by the end of 2003-04. Of them, 47.11 per cent were formed for women. The corresponding proportions for Betul and Chhattarpur were 51.64 and 71.62, respectively. Thus, the proportion of women groups to total SGSY groups tended to be higher in the selected districts as compared to the state.

Gradation of SGSY groups

Gradation is an important component of SGSY programme. The main objective of gradation exercise is to gauge the development status of a SGSY group. The second objective is to identify the weaknesses, if any, and help the group to overcome the same so as to develop into a good group. Grading exercise would, thus, help to focus attention on weak groups so that the implementing agencies can assist the groups to overcome the weaknesses and graduate into good ones. The third objective is to enable the implementing agencies to establish linkages between banks and good groups.

Two rounds of gradation are undertaken – the first one at the end of the formation stage and the second one during the consolidation phase. The formation stage generally lasts six months. At the end of six months, SGSY programme subjects each SHG to a test whether it has evolved into a good group and whether the group is ready to go into the next stage of evolution. Once a group has obtained Grade I, there will be periodical review to assess whether the group has reached a stage at which it could access credit from the banks.

Since DRDAs are expected to play an effective role in the grading exercise, there is provision to improve their capacity in order to undertake this exercise professionally. Grading of the SHGs can be done by the same agency that has been involved in the promotion and development of the SHGs or by an independent agency contracted for this specific purpose. The programme notes that it is desirable to get the grading exercise done by an independent agency, as it will have objectivity and acceptance by financial institutions etc.[2] According to the programme, the grading criteria are to be consistent with the characteristics that are agreed to be essential for strong, self-managed and vibrant SHGs. In other words, the features that a best SHG should have will, therefore, become the starting point of the grading exercise. The following are the processes that are involved in grading exercise.

- Development of one exhaustive list of characteristics of a good group by the DRDA in consultation with its partners, if any, involved in the promotion and development of SHGs.
- Development of criteria for grading of the groups with appropriate weightage for various parameters.
- Identification of suitable agency to undertake grading exercise.
- Intensive training to the investigators who will interact with the members of the group to assess the group on various parameters. This training can either be conducted by the agency identified for grading or by DRDA.
- Facilitating the agency to visit the groups for assessing the development status of the groups.
- Obtaining SHG-wise reports with the rating awarded and the reasons.
- Developing an action plan for each SHG for strengthening the groups identified as weak or average.
- Pursuing with bankers for securing finances to good SHGs under NABARD bank-SHG linkage programme.

Grading exercise should not be a questionnaire-oriented exercise where the members become passive participants. It should provide an opportunity for the members to assess their own performance in a participatory manner. The investigator is expected to assume the role of facilitator in the process. As per the vision, DRDAs should ensure active participation of the bankers in the grading exercise. In this context, NABARD and local banks will have to be involved very closely right from the development of criteria for grading the groups.

As noted earlier, obtaining grade I will entitle a group to access revolving credit fund. The incentive of revolving fund will influence the behaviour of SGSY members in such a manner that they will become responsible in developing self-management principles within their group. In other words, a group passing grade I is supposed to be self-reliant in fixing the agenda for meetings, conducting periodic meetings, electing representatives in a democratic manner and periodic rotation of leadership, and regularity in savings mobilisation. The progress in the number of groups passing through grade I will provide clues on the extent to which the rural development agencies are successful in building self-management principles in the groups.

Grade II is given to those groups which demonstrate that they have acquired the credit discipline. In other words, the group passing through grade II should have disbursed several rounds of credit and have experience in assessing income generating activities for members, disbursement of credit and collecting repayments. The progress in the number of groups passing grade II will indicate the success of the programme in building the capacity of SGSY groups in micro-finance activities.

Table 3.7 shows that the total number of groups passing grade I in a year increased from 1.25 lakhs to 2.05 lakhs during the five-year period. There were year to year fluctuations in the number of groups passing grade I. Of the 48.48 lakh SGSY groups in the country, only 9.10 lakh groups (or only 25.74 per cent) passed grade I during the period of 1999-2000 to 2003-04. This shows very slow progress in the grading process. The proportion of groups passing grade I, which was around 42 per cent in the first two years of the programme gradually declined and reached as low a figure as 11.77 per cent in 2003-04. This suggests the following. First, the programme implementers were giving more emphasis to the formation of SGSY groups rather than their consolidation. Second, notwithstanding the efforts of programme implementers, the groups were unable to pass through the first test probably because the capacity of the programme implementers in this regard was insufficient. Third, the co-ordination (among key actors such as DRDA, SGSY committee, banks, NGOs, etc.) required for grading was not present and hence, a huge gap between groups formed and groups passing through grade I.

Table 3.7: Progress in the Formation and Gradation of SHGs Formed under SGSY Programme (1999-2000 to 2003-2004)

Items	*Years*					
	1999-2000	*2000-01*	*2001-02*	*2002-03*	*2003-04*	*All years*
1. Self-Help groups formed since 1.4.99	292,426	515,691	950,078	1,348,951	1,740,917	4,848,063
2. No. of SHGs passed Grade I	125,402	214,011	176,002	189,634	204,959	910,008
3. Proportion of 2 to 1	42.88	41.5	18.53	14.06	11.77	25.74
4. No. of SHGs passed Grade II	74,234	101,291	54,040	96,020	90,491	416,076
5. Proportion of 4 to 2	59.2	47.33	30.7	50.63	44.15	46.40
6. No. of SHGs which have taken up economic activities	29,017	26,317	30,576	35,317	50,574	171,801
7. Proportion of 6 to 4	39.09	25.98	56.58	36.78	55.89	42.86

Source: Annual Report 2003-04, Ministry of Rural Development, Govt. of India.

The number of SHGs passing grade II was 4.16 lakhs during the five-year period. If one looks at the proportion of grade II SHGs to total number of SGSY groups formed, the percentage is very small at 8.58. However, if one looks at the proportion of grade II SHGs to grade I SHGs, the proportion ranges from as high as 59.2 per cent in 1999-2000 to as low as 30.7 per cent in 2001-02. On the whole, about 46 per cent of grade I SHGs managed to go through grade II test. Apparently, not all groups passing grade II would undertake economic activities. The proportion of groups undertaking economic activities to total SGSY groups was only 3.54 per cent. Thus, only a small proportion of SHGs formed had undertaken economic activities.

Progress in the number of swarojgaris assisted under SGSY programme

The main purpose of SGSY is to facilitate swarojgaris in the rural areas to cross the poverty line. The approach is to make available income generating assets and inputs to the target groups through a package of support services consisting of subsidy and bank loan. Here, the target group consists of small farmers[3], marginal farmers[4], agricultural labourers, non-agricultural labourers and rural artisans whose annual family income was less than Rs.13,000 during 1999-2000.

During the five-year period, 46 lakh swarojgaris were assisted under the programme. The total number obtaining benefits in a year fluctuated between 8 lakhs and 10 lakhs. Of the total number of swarojgaris obtaining benefits during this period, nearly 26 lakh obtained benefits in their individual capacity, while about 20 lakh swarojgaris received the benefits as SHG members. Thus, although the programme aimed to gradually shift to SHG mode, the emphasis was still on individual beneficiaries during the five year period ending with 2003-04. There were, however, indications that the programme was shifting to SHG members. In 1999-2000, the proportion of SHG members receiving benefits to total number of swarojgaris obtaining the benefits was 37.25 per cent, and the proportion gradually increased to 64.33 per cent by 2003-04 (Table 3.8).

Table 3.8: Trends in the Assistance Provided to Swarojgaris (1999-2000 to 2003-2004)

Items	*Years*					
	1999-2000	*2000-01*	*2001-02*	*2002-03*	*2003-04*	*All years*
1. SHGs Swarojgaris assisted	347,912	318,803	364,676	414,419	576,639	2,022,449
2. Individual Swarojgaris assisted	585,956	687,349	572,792	411,848	319,785	2,577,730
3. Total Swarojgaris assisted	933,868	1,006,152	937,468	826,267	896,424	4,600,179
4. Proportion of 1 to 3	37.25	31.69	38.9	50.16	64.33	44.46

Source: *Annual Report 2003-04*, Ministry of Rural Development, Govt. of India.

Across 20 major states, the proportion of swarojgaris receiving benefits was comparatively high in the so-called BIMARU states of Bihar, Madhya Pradesh, Rajasthan and Uttar Pradesh. The proportion of SHG members to total number of swarojgaris assisted was more than 75 per cent in eight states, between 50 to 75 per cent in three states and less than 50 per cent in as many as nine states. In Bihar, the proportion was as low as 14.54 per cent (Table 3.9).

Table 3.9: Distribution (%) of Total Swarojgaris by Major States During 2003-04

States	*SHG Members*	*Individual Swarojgaris*	*Total Number of Swarojgaris Assisted*	*State-wise distribution (%) of swarojgaris*
Andhra Pradesh	80.71	19.29	79,736	8.9
Assam	98.24	1.76	45,480	5.1
Bihar	14.54	85.46	111,613	12.5
Chhatisgarh	23.02	76.98	22,926	2.6
Gujarat	25.65	74.35	21,462	2.4
Haryana	68.90	31.10	11,863	1.3
Himachal Pradesh	72.31	27.69	7,928	0.9
Jammu & Kashmir	38.28	61.72	6,965	0.8
Jharkhand	41.98	58.02	63,173	7.1
Karnataka	86.17	13.83	43,293	4.8
Kerala	68.47	31.53	20,062	2.2
Madhya Pradesh	84.21	15.79	41,979	4.7

(Contd.)

States	SHG Members	Individual Swarojgaris	Total Number of Swarojgaris Assisted	State-wise distribution (%) of Swarojgaris
Madhya Pradesh	84.21	15.79	41,979	4.7
Maharashtra	75.00	25.00	60,659	6.8
Orissa	69.81	30.19	59,289	6.6
Punjab	46.55	53.45	6,554	0.7
Rajasthan	20.85	79.15	28,618	3.2
Tamil Nadu	97.60	2.40	61,120	6.8
Uttar Pradesh	86.67	13.33	140,622	15.7
Uttaranchal	97.76	2.24	10,780	1.2
West Bengal	46.00	54.00	27,008	3.0
India	64.49	35.51	**892,890**	

Source: *Annual Report 2003-04*, Ministry of Rural Development, Govt. of India.

In Madhya Pradesh, the total number of swarojgaris benefiting from the programme was 23,534. In relative terms, Betul accounted for a larger proportion of benefiting swarojgaris (Annex 3.4).

What was the purpose for which the credit was used? The data on the distribution of swarojgaris by the purpose for which the loan was sought shows that the primary sector (consisting of irrigation, land development, milch cattle and others) accounted for over 66 per cent of the loan accounts. The secondary sector (consisting of village industries, handicrafts, handlooms and others) accounted for about 21 per cent.

Within the primary sector, the loans for dairying accounted for a bulk of the loans. In 2003-04, the swarojgaris obtaining loans for the purchase of milch cattle accounted for nearly 37 per cent of the total swarojgaris assisted under the programme. Thus, the SGSY programme focused on primary sector, in general and milch cattle, in particular.

Coverage of disadvantaged groups

The safeguards for SC/ST households have been provided in both physical and financial terms in accordance with central and state government norms. The Government of India norm is 50 per cent

Table 3.10: Distribution of Swarojgaris by Purpose for Which Loan Was Utilised in Major States in India During 2003-2004

Name of the States	*Primary sector*					*Secondary sector*							*Grand total*
	Irrigation	*Land dev.*	*Milch cattle*	*Others*	*Sub-total*	*Village Industries*	*Handicraft*	*Handloom*	*Others*	*Sub-total*	*Others*	*Sub-total*	
Andhra Pradesh	3,560	37,528		5,954	47,042	4,058	1,033	1,468	5,540	12,069		0	59,111
Assam	1,038	18,480	0	12,596	32,114	2,296	1,095	10,651	2,011	16,053		0	48,167
Bihar	5,114		28,458	24,432	58,004	6,673	1,349	664	10,712	19,398	29,914	29,914	107,316
Chhattisgarh	3,363		4,205	6,358	13,926	1,754	179	124	1,469	3,526	5,474	5,474	22,926
Gujarat	1,363		11,773	2,152	15,288	1,139	370	149	1,071	2,729	3,671	3,671	21,688
Haryana	12		15	538	565	187	44	36	881	1,148		0	1,713
Himachal Pradesh	313		4,338	999	5,650	383	43	84	308	818	1,460	1,460	7,928
Jammu & Kashmir	285			491	776	327	2,032	363	168	2,890		0	3,666
Jharkhand	8,679	288		5,732	14,699	2,303	308	335	5,618	8,564		0	23,263
Karnataka	1,460		29,870	5,880	37,210	1,876	504	622	1,110	4,112	1,971	1,971	43,293
Kerala	212		5,785	2,246	8,243	2,564	229	239	2,568	5,600	6,219	6,219	20,062
Madhya Pradesh	7,282		16,330	3,977	27,589	7,892	460	46	1,123	9,521	4,869	4,869	41,979
Maharashtra	3,436		37,897	6,032	47,365	1,997	657	141	1,620	4,415	8,879	8,879	60,659
Orissa	4,329	3,546	12,146	11,531	31,552	11,363	1,067	1,248	2,006	15,684	12,053	12,053	59,289
Punjab	0	7	0	295	302	976	306	579	368	2,229	0	0	2,531
Rajasthan	1,267		16,448	1,953	19,668	768	445	154	1,416	2,783	6,187	6,187	28,638
Tamil Nadu	3,490		32	122,238	15,760	10,523	765	1,513	8,491	21,292		0	37,052
Uttar Pradesh	4,382		102,179	7,197	113,758	8,216	2,132	1,778	5,140	17,266	9,598	9,598	140,622
Uttaranchal	2			1,594	1,596	68	176	49	163	456	0	0	2,052
West Bengal	616		5,997	1,834	8,447	9,183	1,130	730	982	12,025	6,536	6,536	27,008
India	50,367	59,849	285,263	118,439	513,918	74,628	14,420	21,105	53,596	163,749	99,668	99,668	777,335

Source: *Annual Report 2003-04*, Ministry of Rural Development Govt. of India.

for SC and ST households put together. The State norm is 50 per cent for SC households and 10 per cent for ST households (16 per cent in ITDA areas), 40 per cent for women and three per cent for physically challenged beneficiaries. The forum for identification of beneficiary is Grama Sabha. Grama sabha is attended by prospective beneficiaries, representatives of bank, DRDA, block officials, non-officials and village elders.

The proportion of SC/ST swarojgaris assisted under the programme increased gradually from 44.32 per cent in 1990-2000 to 46.12 in 2003-04. During the five-year period of 1999-2000 to 2003-04, 45.32 per cent of swarojgaris assisted under the programme belonged to SC/ST category in the country. The proportion of women swarojgaris obtaining benefits from SGSY increased from 44.62 per cent to 52.41 during this period, while the proportion of disabled persons benefiting from the programme was less than one per cent.

Table 3.11: Disadvantaged Groups Assisted under SGSY Programme (1999-2000 to 2004-2005)

Items	*Years*					
	1999-2000	*2000-01*	*2001-02*	*2002-03*	*2003-04*	*All years*
1. SC Swarojgaris assisted	278,938	310,886	284,040	249,556	275,186	1,398,606
2. ST Swarojgaris assisted	134,944	137,850	143,619	130,260	138,281	684,954
3. SC/ST Swarojgaris assisted	413,882	448,736	427,659	379,816	413,467	2,083,560
4. Women Swarojgaris assisted	416,690	409,842	385,891	382,613	469,824	2,064,860
5. Disabled Swarojgaris assisted	8,529	6,737	6,059	6,118	8,481	35,924
6. %age of SC/STs assisted	44.32	44.6	45.62	45.97	46.12	45.32
7. %age of women assisted	44.62	40.73	41.16	46.31	52.41	45.04
8. %age of disabled assisted	0.91	0.67	0.65	0.74	0.95	0.78

Source: *Annual Report 2003-04*, Ministry of Rural Development, Govt. of India.

The coverage of vulnerable groups across 20 major states has been presented in Table 3.12. The coverage of SC households was the highest in Uttar Pradesh, while it was the least in Jammu & Kashmir. The proportion of ST households obtaining benefits was the highest in Chhattisgarh and nil in Punjab and Haryana. Women constituted over 98 per cent of the swarojgaris assisted during 2003-04, while they constituted only 18.24 per cent in Chhattisgarh (Table 3.12).

In terms of the total number of SHGs formed, this programme was the largest in Madhya Pradesh and the second largest in Karnataka (Annex 1.1). SGSY programme was launched in all the districts in Madhya Pradesh in 1999. As against the target of 100,160 SHGs, 121,643 were formed by March 2002. In the selected districts of Betul and Chhattarpur, the targets were, however, not met. As against the targets of 3,200 and 2,560 SHGs in Betul and Chhattarpur

Table 3.12: Distribution (%) of Swarojgaris by Vulnerability Status (2003-04)

States	*SC*	*ST*	*Women*	*Handi-capped*	*Total Number of Swarojgaris Assisted*
Andhra Pradesh	34.32	9.03	83.79	1.91	79,736
Assam	9.71	19.7	57.62	1.53	45,480
Bihar	35.29	1.66	23.71	0.33	111,613
Chhatisgarh	15.35	42.8	18.24	0.35	22,926
Gujarat	19.35	32.3	38.69	1.65	21,462
Haryana	44.74	0.0	59.08	0.89	11,863
Himachal Pradesh	41.51	10.3	58.1	1.05	7,928
Jammu & Kashmir	5.67	16.8	38.39	0.09	6,965
Jharkhand	16.41	44.9	41.05	0.37	63,173
Karnataka	32.06	8.34	83.53	0.54	43,293
Kerala	36.29	3.0	78.01	1.76	20,062
Madhya Pradesh	27.50	32.3	41.38	1.33	41,979
Maharashtra	27.68	20.1	65.97	1.36	60,659
Orissa	22.82	30.0	65.22	1.31	59,289
Punjab	61.61	0.0	55.45	1.77	6,554
Rajasthan	31.93	17.3	47.64	0.71	28,618
Tamil Nadu	38.57	3.04	98.25	2.04	61,120
Uttar Pradesh	47.03	0.17	31.93	0.45	140,622
Uttaranchal	25.00	4.94	54.46	0.19	10,780
West Bengal	22.16	3.21	47.26	0.06	27,008
India	**30.8**	**15.0**	**52.51**	**0.42**	**892,890**

Source: *Annual Report 2003-04*, Ministry of Rural Development, Govt. of India.

districts, the number of SHGs formed was 3,133 and 1,852 SHGs, respectively by March 2002.

In conclusion, the programme achieved very good results in so far as the formation of groups was concerned. Beginning with 3 lakh groups formed in the first year, the total number of groups formed in a year reached more than 17 lakhs in 2003-04. There were 48.48 lakh SGSY groups in the country by the end of 2003-04.

Gradation is an important exercise in the SGSY programme as this seeks to gauge the development status of the group, rectify the weaknesses if any in the groups and pave the way for linkages with banks. The trends in the progress in the number of groups passing through the grades indicate the development status of the groups. Of the 48.48 lakh SGSY groups in the country, only 9.10 lakh groups (or only 25.74 per cent) passed grade I during the five-year period. This shows very slow progress in the grading process. The proportion of groups passing grade I in each year gradually declined. This suggests the following. First, the programme implementers were giving more emphasis to the formation of SGSY groups rather than their consolidation. Second, there seems to be inadequate capacity of programme implementers to prepare the groups to qualify for the Grade I. Third, the co-ordination (among key actors such as DRDA, SGSY committee, banks, NGOs, etc.) required for grading was not present and hence, a huge gap between groups formed and groups passing through grade I. Even a smaller proportion of SHGs had passed grade II. Apparently, not all the groups passing grade II undertook economic activities. The proportion of the groups undertaking economic activities to total SGSY groups was only 3.54 per cent. Thus, only a small proportion of SHGs formed had undertaken economic activities. It can be, therefore, concluded that although the progress in the formation of groups under the programme was impressive, a large proportion of them did not pass through grade I or grade II required to obtain assistance from the programme.

During the five-year period, 46 lakh swarojgaris obtained benefits from the programme; of them, most received benefits in their individual capacity rather than as group members. Thus, although the programme aimed to gradually shift to SHG mode, the emphasis was still on individual beneficiaries. Most of the assistance provided under the programme was used for agriculture related activities, in general, and for milch cattle, in particular. An analysis of the coverage of members belonging to disadvantaged and vulnerable groups shows that the programme achieved reasonable success, although the coverage of women was lower in a few states.

Factors affecting the performance of SGSY

An analysis of trends in the performance of SGSY was carried out in the previous sections. The indicators such as allocations and utilisation of funds earmarked for the programme, purpose-wise distribution of the financial resources and availability of credit facility to swarojgaris were looked at to analyse the financial progress of the programme. In order to analyse the financial progress of the programme, the aspects covered were progress in the formation and gradation of SGSY groups, number of swarojgaris assisted and coverage of swarojgaris belonging to disadvantaged and vulnerable groups.

The main conclusions emerging from the discussion in the previous two sections have been summarised at the end of each section. Key conclusions on the performance of SGSY programme have been recapitulated below so that the contributing factors can be analysed.

- The releases towards the programme implementation fell short of the allocations.
- The programme could not utilise the funds available for different programme.
- While the utilisation of the amount budgeted for disbursal of subsidy constantly increased that on infrastructure development and skill provision remained low.

- The targets fixed for mobilisation of credit could not be achieved.
- Subsidy disbursal was largely for individual swarojgaris rather than to SHG members.
- The progress in the formation of groups was spectacular. The number of groups formed in the country was over 48 lakhs by 2003-04.
- About one-fourth of 48 lakh groups passed through grade I. And much less proportion of groups passed grade II. grade I indicates that the group is strong, while grade II indicates that the group has acquired credit discipline. The low proportions of groups passing through grades indicate the failure of the programme in the consolidation of groups formed under the programme.

What factors affected the performance of the programme? In the ensuing paragraphs, an attempt has been made to analyse the factors affecting the performance of SGSY programme with the help of available studies and government reports.

Low central releases

SGSY programme places considerable emphasis on group approach. The theories on group dynamics suggest that the groups should be formed only after mobilising the poor. Such mobilisation is to be based on an understanding of the situation and the needs of the poor. If the exercise is carried out by an external agency on its own, there is a problem of costs as well as lack of ownership among the intended beneficiaries on the very process itself. Hence, participatory methods have been suggested to both social mobilisation of the poor and in the formation of groups. The groups for micro-finance should be small in size and homogenous. This essentially implies that the role to be played by the intervening agency should be that of facilitator and not of implementers. The agency in question should also have not only the required expertise in social mobilisation through participatory methods but also a

belief in the participatory processes. The whole task of formation and consolidation of groups should not be viewed as target-oriented but as a process where the beneficiaries participate in all aspects relating to these two tasks.

SGSY recognises that the staff in the line departments is not equipped to undertake the task of formation and consolidation of groups. Hence, it suggests that the help of NGOs be taken for this task, and has made specific provisions for selecting NGOs, community based organisations, societies, etc., for this purpose. The idea is that NGOs would accompany the SGSY groups for a period of 2-3 years and mould the groups of poor into self-managed institutions (GoI 2004).

It appears that the DRDAs faced problems in the identification of suitable NGOs for undertaking the tasks of the formation of SGSY groups. The Tenth Five-Year Plan notes that two factors contributed for low central releases. First, lack of requisite skills within DRDA in social mobilisation. It has been observed that "field officers were not in a position to organise self-help groups which could be provided financial assistance" (GoI 2002c: 295). Second, the NGOs, which could organise SHGs, were not in place. It may be noted that the NGO movement is characterised by patchwork quilt phenomenon (Rajasekhar 2000). The large, influential and well-funded NGOs did not concentrate resources in regions and sectors that were most important for national development (Robinson 1993). This was found to be happening in India. Although human and economic development indicators were better in south India as compared to the central Indian states of Bihar, Madhya Pradesh, parts of Uttar Pradesh and western state of Rajasthan, the concentration of NGOs was more in the former as compared to the latter. This is borne by the fact that out of 12,136 organisations receiving foreign funding and reporting to the Home Ministry in 1996-97, there were 5,721 organisations in south India, while the number was only 1,779 in the BIMARU region (Kumar 1999: 16).

The Working Group on poverty alleviation programmes for the Tenth Five-Year Plan provides two additional factors for low

central releases. First, much of the time was spent on preparatory work and sensitisation of functionaries at various levels and bankers. This implies that the programme of national magnitude was launched without sufficient preparation. This caused enormous delays in the formation of groups, which could be provided with financial assistance. Second, a lot of time was required for the formation of SHGs, their capacity building and gradation (GoI 2001). This implies that the SGSY programme should be implemented as a process-oriented one. While this point is well taken, one cannot understand why budgetary provision was made for the disbursal of subsidy and targets were fixed for credit mobilisation.

Evidence also suggests that even when NGOs were present, it was not necessary that there was collaboration between government and NGOs due to the following reasons. First, there was antagonistic relationship. Rajasekhar and Biradar (2004) note that the relationship between government and NGOs was of three types; collaboration, co-option in the guise of collaboration and critical collaboration. The evidence on GO-NGO collaboration gathered by Rajasekhar and Biradar (2004) shows that the government agencies were willing to collaborate with NGOs only when the relationship was characterised by co-option and simple collaboration. But not when the NGOs wanted critical collaboration. Second, whenever there was collaboration between NGOs and government in the implementation of SGSY programme, the relationship was marked by several difficulties. Untimely release of funds and bureaucratic approach to collaboration came in the way of good and successful NGOs to partner with the government in the formation and consolidation of SGSY groups (Box 3.1). The NGO in this case was reasonably successful in consolidating the groups and linking them with banks. Even then government agencies could not undertake timely monitoring, resulting in considerable delay in the release of funds. Hence, the NGO stopped collaborating with the government agency.

Box 3.1: Urmul Khejri: In the Quagmire of SGSY

Urmul Khejri is a sister organisation of Urmul Trust which was registered in 1998. Urmul Khejri started to collaborate with the government in 2002 for implementing the SGSY programme. According to the contract, the NGO was to form and sustain 30 SHGs in a two-year period. The funding support was to the tune of Rs.10,000 per group, and the instalments would be released as per the progress stipulated in the contract. By 2003, the NGO could ensure that two groups had passed grade two and had to be linked to the bank. But, the linkages with the bank could not be established. According to the NGO, the SGSY committee was not regular in its monitoring function. The government was blaming the banks for not sanctioning money to the group. After getting distressed with the tidy pace of progress, the NGO was stopped from forming groups because of not getting enough funds for the staff. This NGO was also collaborating with NABARD in implementing a similar scheme. Though it was getting Rs.1,800 per group in comparison to Rs.10,000 from the government under SGSY programme, the things were reported to be smooth in the case of collaboration with NABARD because of regular monitoring and sanction of funds.

Source: Panda 2004.

Low credit mobilisation

Several factors have contributed for low credit mobilisation. It has been pointed out by a study undertaken in Gujarat that there was hiatus between the vision and actual practice (Sud 2003). The study locates the problems in the implementation at the village, state and national levels. At the state level the emphasis was on forming SHGs on target basis. Directives were issued to district and block level staff to form as many groups in as short a time as possible. This burdened the village level worker, who was pressurised to form SHGs in a very hasty manner. This ultimately resulted in the adoption of target-oriented approach and completely ignoring the participatory processes as proposed in the programme guidelines.

The groups that were hastily formed did not naturally have any cohesiveness within the group. Mandhotra and Bhan (2003) found that the main motive in joining the SHGs was to access the credit and subsidy from the bank. The village level worker had the motivation to form as many groups as possible to reach the target. Against this background, the groups formed were lacking in self-management. The attendance in meetings was poor and savings were irregular. The records were maintained for the sole purpose of making information available for banks to grade them. Hence, the records were found to be fake. Further, the process of internal loaning was found to be a fake exercise mainly to get good score in the grading for availing subsidy. Thus, the records did not achieve the primary purpose intended of them, namely, to improve transparency and accountability to the members. This, in turn, resulted in poor cohesiveness within the group and lack of dynamism.

When banks found some of these problems, they were reluctant to extend credit facility to SGSY groups. Even when the groups were genuine, the problems of inadequate staff within banks and lack of co-ordination between government agencies and lending institutions resulted in poor performance in so far as achieving the targets on credit mobilisation.

Slow progress in passing through grades

As noted earlier, grades I and II indicate the success of a group in acquiring self-management and inculcation of credit discipline. Many groups could graduate to the stage where they could demonstrate that they had acquired self-management. Consequently, about 25 per cent of the total groups formed could pass through grade I. There were, however, problems when it came to grade II. This was because of the following reasons.

- SGSY aims at the selection of income generating activities based on a cluster approach and through a consultative and participatory process. As per the programme,

participants should be actively involved in decision-making. The traditional knowledge of the SHG members should be combined with technical knowledge of block level SGSY committee in the selection of suitable activities. Sud (2003: 4086), however, found that SGSY members had very different ideas on what they wanted to do with the loan. The village level staff made women members to believe that they could take up any income generation activity that they wished to. The perception of the staff was, on the other hand, that the women knew nothing about income generating activities and they were like 'blank pieces of paper'. Such perceptual differences resulted in non-participatory or top-down approach in the selection of activities. When women did not own the activities that were selected, it was difficult for the group to pass through grade II.

- The lower awareness about basic features of the programme was found among participating members, especially, those belonging to BPL households (Sen *et al* 2002a and 2000b). These studies have also found out several lacuna in the selection of beneficiaries and activities, capacity building and decision-making process. All these have contributed to the inability of the groups to pass through grades.
- Problems were also noticed in the functioning of banks. As per the design, the banks were expected to play a major role in providing credit facilities. The design also stipulates multiple doses of credit rather than providing credit at one time. This implies that Swarojgaris would get second and subsequent doses of credit only when they demonstrated that they had properly utilised the assets provided during the first round and the first loan was repaid. The Working Group on poverty alleviation programmes for the Tenth Five Year Plan found inadequate appreciation of objectives of SGSY and advantages of group finance by field level bankers and inadequate delegation of power to bank branches to sanction loan beyond a certain amount (GoI 2001).

ANNEX 3.1

Finances (Rs. in lakhs) Provided to SGSY Programme in Madhya Pradesh - A District-wise Picture

District	Total alloca-tion	Balance as on 1.4.2004	Releases by		Other receipt	Total available funds	Expenditure								% of exp.
			Central	State			Subsidy	Revolv-ing fund	Infrastru-cture dev.	Training	Capacity building	Risk fund	Other	Total	
Badwani	171	80	64	21	0	166	12	7	13	0	0	0	0	32	19
Balaghat	393	4	147	26	2	179	128	23	31	6	10	0	1	202	100
Betul	190	57	71	24	5	156	117	14	11	5	1	0	6	155	99
Bhind	94	2	35	12	0	49	37	6	0	0	5	0	0	48	98
Bhopal	50	0	19	6	0	25	18	3	5	3	0	0	0	29	100
Chhatarpur	194	9	73	24	0	106	72	9	1	1	3	0	12	106	100
Chhindwara	275	24	103	39	1	166	56	17	33	12	16	0	0	134	80
Damoh	214	53	80	27	0	160	27	2	22	0	9	0	0	60	37
Datia	29	33	11	4	0	47	18	4	1	3	0	0	0	26	54
Dewas	142	5	53	18	10	85	72	6	2	0	1	2	0	83	97
Dhar	218	24	82	27	8	141	71	6	14	1	1	0	0	93	66
Dindori	146	18	55	18	2	92	31	6	17	0	3	0	0	65	69
Guna	221	22	83	28	0	132	50	12	10	15	4	0	0	99	74
Gwalior	83	6	31	10	10	58	86	3	0	0	0	0	0	89	100
Harda	51	0	19	6	2	28	33	3	0	0	1	0	0	37	100
Hoshangabad	110	10	41	14	11	75	29	8	13	7	0	0	0	58	77
Indore	61	5	23	8	2	38	47	2	7	2	5	0	0	63	100
Jabalpur	257	9	96	35	19	159	131	9	18	0	2	0	0	159	100
Jhabua	251	14	94	31	3	142	61	10	23	6	1	0	0	101	71

(Contd.)

District	Total allocation	Balance as on. 1.4.2004	Releases by		Other receipt	Total available funds	Expenditure								% of exp.
			Central	State			Subsidy	Revolving fund	Infrastructure dev.	Training	Capacity building	Risk fund	Other	Total	
Katani	240	1	90	15	1	107	76	32	11	0	2	0	0	121	100.0
Khandwa	216	1	81	27	13	122	91	9	7	9	0	0	0	115	94.0
Khargone	181	5	68	23	0	95	72	20	16	2	0	0	0	109	100.0
Mandla	242	20	91	30	5	146	49	10	38	8	0	0	0	111	76.3
Mandsour	114	0	43	14	3	60	49	6	6	3	0	0	0	65	100.0
Morena	90	2	34	11	16	63	58	2	0	0	0	0	0	60	96.2
Narsinghpur	173	0	65	22	2	89	22	14	13	0	9	0	0	58	64.5
Nimach	60	1	22	7	0	31	16	13	2	0	1	0	0	31	100.0
Panna	166	1	62	21	1	85	44	7	15	5	3	0	0	73	86.2
Raisen	194	10	73	24	0	107	53	10	4	3	3	0	0	73	67.8
Rajgarh	174	4	65	22	16	107	43	0	21	7	0	0	0	70	65.5
Ratlam	116	18	44	15	2	79	56	8	3	1	1	0	0	68	86.3
Rewa	460	23	173	58	0	253	42	9	13	0	0	0	0	64	25.3
Sagar	324	54	122	41	0	216	27	4	15	2	0	0	0	51	23.6
Satna	342	4	128	43	0	174	125	46	27	6	6	0	0	212	100.0
Sehore	117	1	44	15	12	71	69	7	2	1	6	0	0	86	100.0
Seoni	227	0	85	28	1	114	49	25	8	0	11	0	0	94	82.7
Shahdol	243	26	91	30	2	149	65	4	0	0	4	0	0	73	49.0
Shajapur	139	7	52	17	7	84	44	25	6	5	1	0	0	83	99.8
Shivpuri	136	13	51	17	0	81	49	2	14	0	0	0	0	64	79.3
Shyopur Kala	62	6	23	7	0	36	16	4	4	2	0	0	0	25	69.4
Sidhi	362	42	136	45	0	223	91	19	27	0	9	0	0	145	65.3
Tikamgarh	145	21	55	19	0	94	37	12	20	0	1	0	0	79	83.8
Ujjain	115	1	43	14	1	60	37	4	7	3	3	0	0	55	92.4
Umariya	77	2	30	8	4	43	20	3	8	0	3	0	0	34	80.4
Vidisha	144	1	54	18	2	75	56	7	5	0	0	0	0	74	98.8
State	**8,011**	**636**	**3,005**	**967**	**161**	**4,769**	**2,450**	**450.4**	**511.5**	**117.1**	**123.3**	**2.3**	**18.6**	**3,734**	**78.31**

ANNEX 3.2

Credit Mobilised in Madhya Pradesh During 2003-04 (Rs. in lakhs)

District	Total credit mobilisation			% of achievement	Credit mobilised to		% credit Mobilised to SHGs	Per capita investment (in Rs.)
	Credit	Subsidy	Total		SHGs	Individual		
Badwani	26	12	38	10.67	36	2	94.9	22,857
Balaghat	323	128	451	55.71	407	44	90.2	52,027
Betul	306	117	423	100.00	423	0	100.0	36,452
Bhind	62	37	99	48.68	98	1	990	29,852
Bhopal	70	18	88	77.06	75	13	84.9	40,691
Chhatarpur	69	72	142	34.82	142	0	100.0	35,363
Chhindwara	111	56	168	29.36	168	0	100.0	28,485
Damoh	47	27	74	16.61	74	0	100.0	49,073
Datia	55	18	73	100.00	73	0	100.0	39,360
Dewas	202	72	274	90.92	274	0	100.0	40,876
Dhar	120	71	190	41.83	190	0	100.0	39,956
Dindori	41	31	72	23.43	62	11	85.2	32,518
Guna	69	50	120	25.96	115	5	96.0	39,990
Gwalior	214	86	300	100.00	299	2	99.5	31,407
Harda	67	33	100	85.52	100	0	100.0	38,137
Hoshangabad	63	29	92	38.85	87	5	95.1	30,909
Indore	93	47	140	100.00	128	11	92.1	30,130
Jabalpur	162	131	293	54.89	265	28	90.5	38,607
Jhabua	103	61	163	31.39	144	20	87.8	34,840
Katani	363	76	439	88.06	356	83	81.1	38,868
Khandwa	284	91	375	83.26	205	170	54.6	39,503

(Contd.)

District	Total credit mobilisation			% of achievement	Credit mobilised to		% credit Mobilised to SHGs	Per capita investment (in Rs.)
	Credit	Subsidy	Total		SHGs	Individual		
Khargone	200	72	271	71.33	271	0	100.0	31,412
Mandla	83	49	132	26.18	132	0	100.0	29,102
Mandsour	113	49	162	66.23	124	38	76.6	25,986
Morena	120	58	178	91.25	178	0	100.0	32,052
Narsinghpur	39	22	61	16.83	61	0	100.0	28,654
Nimach	29	16	45	33.56	39	6	87.7	7,443
Panna	55	44	99	28.21	99	0	100.0	25,107
Raisen	133	53	185	45.54	148	37	79.9	40,610
Rajgarh	208	43	251	68.53	250	1	99.5	56,580
Ratlam	104	56	159	64.11	159	0	100.0	44,144
Rewa	126	42	167	17.73	167	0	100.0	44,055
Sagar	64	27	90	13.52	42	48	47.0	43,287
Satna	230	125	355	50.39	353	2	99.3	39,130
Sehore	231	69	300	100.00	292	8	97.2	49,654
Seoni	135	49	184	39.01	184	0	100.0	35,589
Shahdol	159	65	224	44.38	224	1	99.7	30,404
Shajapur	130	44	175	59.47	161	14	92.2	29,639
Shivpuri	135	49	184	63.57	179	5	97.6	37,607
Shyopur Kala	26	16	42	30.30	42	0	100.0	14,705
Sidhi	111	91	202	27.06	202	0	100.0	24,165
Tikamgarh	39	37	77	24.97	77	0	100.0	9,850
Ujjain	153	37	190	77.15	190	1	99.7	33,329
Umariya	45	20	65	38.28	65	0	100.0	26,356
Vidisha	119	56	175	57.45	172	3	98.4	44,382
Total	5,637	2,450	8,087	**48.10**	7,530	557	**93.1**	**34,365**

ANNEX 3.3

No. of SHGs Formed

District	*No. of SHGs formed (Cumulative)*	*No. of SHGs formed during the year*	*No. of women SHGs*	*Financial target loan + subsidy (Rs. in lakhs)*
Badwani	4,946	161	3,118	359.72
Balaghat	7,439	1,770	4,152	808.75
Betul	3,311	0	1,710	396.94
Bhind	3,292	0	598	203.58
Bhopal	1,382	64	537	114.59
Chhatarpur	4,060	0	2,908	406.19
Chhindwara	3,618	0	1,631	570.55
Damoh	4,709	0	1,642	446.03
Datia	976	36	247	71.95
Dewas	6,378	131	2,020	300.76
Dhar	10,466	7	6,761	454.73
Dindori	3,091	223	1,083	308.06
Guna	7,223	0	4,165	460.60
Gwalior	2,607	82	1,405	180.88
Harda	1,144	0	442	117.28
Hoshangabad	4,328	55	2,290	236.27
Indore	3,775	0	1,331	137.24
Jabalpur	10,016	136	3,104	533.13
Jhabua	6,532	0	4,822	520.62
Katani	4,692	7	1,648	498.78
Khandwa	9,823	0	4,041	450.27
Khargone	14,854	63	5,148	380.46
Mandla	5,956	72	2,987	503.64
Mandsour	4,543	11	2,070	244.83
Morena	3,883	76	1,064	194.95
Narsinghpur	3,017	244	825	364.33
Nimach	2,708	32	1,792	134.16
Panna	4,569	59	1,498	349.83
Raisen	4,696	89	2,212	406.64
Rajgarh	2,803	152	1,447	365.75
Ratlam	8,392	581	4,686	248.56
Rewa	4,414	13	2,288	944.06
Sagar	3,483	130	910	669.08
Satna	6,539	1,128	2,557	704.30
Sehore	3,810	70	1,370	250.09
Seoni	5,466	1,281	2,455	472.58
Shahdol	16,498	0	12,213	505.55
Shajapur	4,989	444	2,202	294.06
Shivpuri	4,382	0	460	289.30
Shyopur Kala	2,593	56	458	138.30
Sidhi	5,854	390	3,410	745.78
Tikamgarh	2,433	0	1,356	307.70
Ujjain	6,297	84	3,147	246.68
Umariya	3,198	16	2,487	170.08
Vidisha	3,050	600	701	305.17
TOTAL	**232,235**	**8,263**	**109,398**	**16812.8**

ANNEX 3.4

Physical Progress

District	*Physical progress*				
	S.C.	*S.T.*	*Women*	*Disabled*	*No. of benefiting households*
Badwani	0.0	88.1	11.9	0.0	168
Balaghat	9.2	19.1	59.1	7.2	866
Betul	12.8	52.2	59.1	0.3	1,159
Bhind	47.0	0.0	32.2	0.3	332
Bhopal	43.3	6.9	40.1	0.5	217
Chhatarpur	42.5	3.3	51.3	0.0	400
Chhindwara	9.2	48.3	57.3	0.2	588
Damoh	9.3	29.1	39.1	0.0	151
Datia	40.3	0.0	44.1	0.0	186
Dewas	34.4	27.7	56.7	0.0	669
Dhar	6.9	71.2	42.2	0.2	476
Dindori	0.0	84.7	46.8	4.5	222
Guna	38.1	24.4	25.4	5.7	299
Gwalior	36.9	13.7	46.1	0.6	956
Harda	19.0	56.7	44.9	0.0	263
Hoshangabad	21.5	51.9	72.4	4.4	297
Indore	21.4	32.0	35.2	6.7	463
Jabalpur	11.2	27.6	25.9	3.2	758
Jhabua	3.6	96.4	59.7	0.0	469
Katani	13.4	43.8	34.1	4.2	1,130
Khandwa	12.4	36.4	49.0	1.3	949
Khargone	24.1	45.7	33.4	1.2	864
Mandla	7.9	64.2	45.9	1.3	453
Mandsour	38.8	2.2	40.5	5.1	624
Morena	25.9	4.0	35.0	0.4	555
Narsinghpur	16.4	16.4	22.0	0.0	214
Nimach	26.1	11.2	57.9	4.8	605
Panna	14.5	6.6	28.2	0.0	393
Raisen	24.1	26.8	36.6	19.7	456
Rajgarh	22.3	7.4	44.9	0.5	443
Ratlam	22.7	24.9	36.3	2.8	361
Rewa	32.9	26.8	50.3	0.0	380
Sagar	43.5	17.7	38.3	1.0	209
Satna	22.6	23.2	47.4	0.0	907
Sehore	39.7	14.2	53.3	5.8	604
Seoni	17.8	23.7	65.6	0.2	518
Shahdol	8.1	54.9	60.0	0.3	738
Shajapur	50.7	0.5	51.7	3.4	590
Shivpuri	37.2	17.8	39.5	2.7	489
Shyopur Kala	12.6	70.2	75.4	0.0	285
Sidhi	20.0	29.9	20.6	0.8	835
Tikamgarh	46.2	5.1	69.2	2.6	780
Ujjain	52.9	1.8	39.2	1.2	571
Umariya	3.6	58.7	75.3	0.0	247
Vidisha	65.6	5.8	11.1	0.0	395
TOTAL	24.2	29.6	45.7	2.2	**23,534**

NOTES

1. Subsidy will be back-ended. Banks would disburse the full project cost including subsidy to the Swarojgaris as loan. The benefits of subsidy will also be available to Swarojgaris who prefer to avail themselves of required working capital in the form of cash credit. The operation of subsidy amount by the bank will be as follows: The subsidy admissible to the Swarojgaris under SGSY should be kept in the Subsidy Reserve Fund Account Swarojgari-wise instead of in terms of deposit in the name of the Swarojgari. Banks should apply no interest on the Subsidy Reserve Fund Account. In view of this, for the purpose of charging interest on the loan, the subsidy amount should be excluded. The balance lying to the credit of Subsidy Reserve Fund Account will not form part of DTL for the purpose of SLR/CRR. In the case of Working Capital advances also, subsidy may be kept in the Reserve Fund Account as stated above without any interest being offered. However, the amount standing to the credit of the account should be withdrawn and credited to a Cash Credit Account of the SGSY Swarojgaris after a period of 5 years. The repayment schedule of loan would be drawn in such a way that the subsidy kept under subsidy Reserve Fund would be sufficient for adjustment towards the last few installments. Swarojgaris will not be entitled for any benefit of subsidy, if the loan is fully repaid before a certain fixed period specified by NABARD depending upon the activity. The availability of the benefit of subsidy to Swarojgaris would be contingent on their proper utilization of loan as also its prompt repayment and maintaining the asset in good condition.
2. A number of government and NGO agencies, working with SHGs across the country have evolved very effective strategies for grading the SHGs. The same could be utilised for the grading exercise.
3. Small farmers are those having land holding from 2.5 to 5.0 acres dry land in non-DPAP areas or 3.75 to 7.5 acres dry land in DPAP areas or half the limits in case of wet land.
4. Marginal farmers are those having land holding up to 2.5 acres in non-DPAP areas or 3.75 acres in DPAP areas in terms of dry land or half the limits in case of wet lands.

4

Conceptual Framework and Research Methodology

Introduction

Development may be seen as a process by which options are increasingly available to the poor to have access to resources towards improving their living conditions (Rajasekhar 2004). Development aims to create a socio-economic order in which the basic needs of everyone are satisfied and where a constant progress towards equity is made (Todaro 1977). Development interventions will become most effective and appropriate if they are based on an understanding of poverty (dimensions and causes), and strategies pursued by the poor and development actors to combat poverty. Any intervention on poverty alleviation requires a thorough understanding of the processes that generate poverty. Such an intervention will have a good chance of success when it is designed on the basis of situation and needs of the poor. A poverty alleviation project must be able to answer the following questions before it is designed: Who are the poor? Why are they poor? What means do they adopt to overcome poverty? Which are the organisations involved in poverty alleviation in the locality? How to design an action plan by taking situation and needs of the poor into consideration? How will one involve government officials and representatives of local decentralised government in the discussions on development of action plans? It is, thus, necessary to analyse the situation of the poor and assess their needs before a project is designed.

Decentralisation and Poverty Alleviation

What is the role of central and state governments in reducing poverty? Poverty anywhere in the country is the concern of both central and local governments and hence, they have to take part in poverty alleviation. Central government's intervention is necessary to ensure optimal resource allocation for redistribution (Brown and Oates 1987; Ladd and Doolittle 1982). Thus, redistribution of income has been traditionally considered to be the responsibility of the central government.

It is, however, important to note that different regions may have different needs and preferences for poverty alleviation, and different capacities to meet these needs and preferences[1]. Experience has shown that sub-central governments do play an important role in the design and implementation of poverty alleviation strategy (Pauly 1973; Ladd and Doolittle 1982; Brown and Oates 1987). Further, sub-central governments do undertake significant amount of redistribution activity even when their efficiency is seen to be doubtful (Oates 1999). Thus, sub-national governments do in fact play a significant role in direct poverty alleviation.

It is now believed that a successful poverty alleviation strategy in any country has four distinct elements. First, it is necessary to identify the poor and know what their characteristics are. Second, it is important to understand the reasons and the factors that contribute to poverty. Once the poor are identified and the causes of poverty are known, it is possible to determine the third element of the strategy, namely, designing a set of specific policies to improve the living conditions of the poor. An effective strategy to improve the living standards of the poor requires measures to accelerate growth (capacity improving) as well as those which directly enhance their immediate consumption entitlements (safety net). Even in growth accelerating policies, it is possible to bias the growth to ensure greater benefits to the poor. Finally, the implementation of these policies should be cost efficient and effective and the institutions evolved to implement them should ensure that the policies benefit the intended target groups (Rao 2002).

The above implies that the governments that are 'closer to the people' should be, in principle, able to provide services more efficiently and effectively than a remote and central authority. The proximity of the local government to the people reduces information and transaction costs in designing and implementing anti-poverty strategy significantly. Local governments, thus, have a distinct advantage in identifying the poor due to their proximity to the people (Rao 2002).

For the local governments to be effective in the design and implementation of anti-poverty programmes, the following need to be present.

- Assignment of responsibilities between different levels of government should be appropriate and the system of inter-governmental transfers should produce right type of incentives (Bird 1993).
- In places where poverty is concentrated, standards of physical and social services provided are low, resulting in low productivity of both capital (including land) and labour. The transfer system should ensure that poorer localities have adequate resources to deliver the desired 'package' of services without adversely affecting their incentive structure (Rao and Das Gupta 1995).
- In order to increase the stakes of local governments in anti-poverty programmes, it is desirable to make the local residents bear a part of the cost of such programmes. Thus, for reasons of efficiency in the delivery mechanism and to ensure greater accountability, it is necessary to have a co-operative solution – a cost sharing programme between the central and local governments in anti-poverty interventions. The analysis shows that the poor are concentrated in poor regions. In a multilevel fiscal system, however, the solutions to poverty alleviation problem have to be found within the principles of co-operative

federalism. This implies that the central government will have to find much of the resources for poverty alleviation programmes whereas the local governments will undertake actual design and implementation of these programmes. This makes intergovernmental transfers an important policy instrument tool in the poverty alleviation strategy. General purpose of transfers should be designed to offset fiscal disabilities of poorer regions. This enables them to provide social and physical infrastructure at levels comparable to those in richer jurisdictions at equivalent tax rates. Such transfers enable the depressed regions to fully utilise their growth potential and accelerated growth in these regions will hasten poverty reduction (Rao 2002).

- The level of decentralisation also plays an important role in the ability of local government to design and implement poverty alleviation programme. If elected leaders do not have control over development personnel, the design and implementation may suffer. Similarly, the low level of fiscal decentralisation may also hamper the ability of local government in the implementation of anti-poverty programmes.

SGSY programme, the details of which were discussed in Chapter 2, is an example where the local government is entrusted with the responsibility of implementing the programme. Panchayat Raj institutions at all the three levels have been assigned the responsibility of monitoring and evaluation. The Grama Sabha is entrusted with the responsibility of conflict resolution and accountability. By assigning these functions to local government, the policy makers assume that the local government contributes to the success of the programme.

Another interesting aspect is that SGSY programme is different as compared to other similar programmes undertaken in the past. In this programme, the rural poor (especially women) are organised into SHGs, the formation of which has been entrusted to the department of rural development. If the department chooses, it can take the help of NGOs in the formation. Second, the SHG members are expected to meet at periodic intervals to discuss common issues such as acquisition of skills, gaining access to credit, undertaking of income generating activities, solving problems faced in income generation and so on. Third, the SHGs are required to mobilise savings, establish linkages with the banks to avail credit from them and arrive at collective decisions regarding income generation programmes. Fourth, linkages between SGSY groups, on the one hand, and local elected bodies, line departments, on the other, are envisaged. As per the design, the Zilla panchayat approves key economic activities and reviews the programme, while the Taluk Panchayat approves the list of economic activities to be undertaken at the cluster level. The Grama Panchayat is expected to undertake the functions of monitoring and ensuring repayment. The Grama Sabha approves the list of households identified for the inclusion in SGSY group and identifies activities to be undertaken at the village level.

The above design raises a number of questions. Can the people participate in the formation of groups, meetings, savings contribution and in establishing linkages? The studies show that the member and household characteristics, the village and group characteristics and institutional features enable or disable members' participation. Is it possible for the line department to form quality groups? In the past, the line department was entrusted with the responsibility of group formation. In such cases, the groups formed were not always homogenous and qualitative. This was attributed to lack of incentives for the line department staff. Further, the resources (human and financial) allocated for the group formation were inadequate, and stiff targets were assigned for the group formation. Inadequate resources and target chasing resulted in the formation of heterogeneous groups. Because of limited time available, participatory methodologies in the group formation could not be adopted and the influential persons in the village were approached for help in this regard. This, in turn, led to the dominance of local elite in the groups formed at the village level. The members (especially the poor and illiterate women) also could not improve their access to credit for reasons such as widespread perception among them that credit for income generation was inherently risky, neglect of credit plus activities, linking savings with credit, and overemphasis on linkages with banks for obtaining credit.

The SGSY programme places considerable emphasis on linkages among development actors at the village level for implementation, resource mobilisation, ensuring that the processes (participation, transparency and accountability) adopted are qualitative and achieving good development outcomes (equity, effectiveness and sustainability). A key question is that whether the linkages work? The women belonging to poorer households face several problems relating to their day-to-day livelihood and hence, face constraints in establishing linkages. Distant location between their place of residence and location of line department, banks, etc., also comes in the way. Complicated procedures and indifferent attitude of the bankers, officials, etc., are also constraints.

In this context, the following questions arise. What have been the processes followed in the implementation of SGSY? Did the programme succeed in mobilising poor women in the formation of SGSY groups, meetings and savings contribution? What was their participation in planning for income generation and borrowing from the groups? What were the linkages between SGSY groups consisting of poor women and decentralised government/line department/banks? How many poor women mobilised assistance from banks? Did the elected local bodies participate in the programme? If yes, what was the nature of their participation? If not, what factors contributed to their limited participation? Since the programme was implemented only from 1999 onwards, it may be too early to analyse the impact of the programme in terms of employment generation, asset creation and income increase. Nevertheless, one question that can be asked is: Is the programme on track in so far as achieving the objectives of enabling the poor to undertake self-employment activities for poverty reduction is concerned?

Hypotheses

- The attributes of promoting agencies and village characteristics influence the homogeneity of groups.
- Village and household characteristics influence members' participation in savings and credit programmes.
- The status of decentralisation influences the linkages between Grama panchayats and SGSY groups.
- There is an association between village and household characteristics, and linkages between banks and SGSY groups.

Indicators and Variables

In order to analyse the above hypotheses, the study identified indicators and variables (Chart 4.1).

Chart 4.1: Identified Indicators and Variables

Indicators	Variables
Adequacy of human resources	• Index on human and material resources in the promoting agencies
Socio-economic homogeneity of groups	• Proportion of ST/SC members in a group • Gini ratio on landholdings of members
Village characteristics	• Size of the village • Proportion of ST/SC in a village • Proportion of very poor and poor in a village • Distance of a village to nearby town
Household and member characteristics	• Caste of the household • Landholding of the household • Education of the member • Income of the household
Participation in savings and credit	• Amount (Rs.) saved by the members • Number of meetings attended by the members • Amount borrowed by the members

(Contd.)

Indicators	Variables
Political, administrative and fiscal decentralisation	• Perceptions of panchayat presidents on their ability to make decisions • Perceptions of grama panchayat presidents on whether the development administration reports them
	• Proportion of own revenue to total revenue in the grama panchayats • Proportion of transfers from the government to the total budget
Number and quality of linkages	• Perceptions of households on number and quality of linkages

Sample Size

The primary data were extracted from the database built for the World Bank project on Roles of Rural Local Organisations in Development Projects. The household data used in this study pertained to 19 SGSY groups located in Betul and Chhattarpur districts of Madhya Pradesh. In addition, data were also collected from the representatives of SGSY groups, grama panchayats and staff of line department. A separate visit was undertaken to the study districts to collect additional secondary data, and to conduct interviews with key stakeholders such as the District Collector, Chief Executive Officer and Block Development Officer. Further, qualitative information from the groups was also collected.

In all, data were collected from 147 households having membership in SGSY groups. The households were randomly selected after obtaining a list of members in the SGSY group. The study also came across defunct SGSY groups. Even in these cases, the data from members of defunct groups were collected to identify the factors contributing to the failure of SGSY programme.

Area Description

Betul and Chhattarpur are vastly different in their location and historical legacy. Betul is located on the southern boarder of the

State and has Maratha culture. On the other hand, Chhattarpur is located in the Bundelkhand region, bordering Uttar Pradesh in the north eastern side.

Table 4.1 provides basic details of the selected districts. In terms of total geographical area, Betul is larger than Chhattarpur. Although the total population was larger in Betul as compared to Chhattarpur, the density of population was lower in the former. This was despite the fact that the population growth during 1991-2000 was higher in Betul as compared to Chhattarpur.

In terms of women development, the indicators from Betul show that the district was more developed. The sex ratio was more in favour of women in Betul as compared to Chhattarpur. In fact, the sex ratio in Betul was higher than the State average. The improved status of women was also reflected in literacy rates. The literacy rate for the entire district was 67 in Betul, while it was 53 in Chhattarpur. In so far as female literacy rate was concerned, Betul was far better as compared to Chhattarpur. The Human Development Report compiled by the Madhya Pradesh government also shows that gender development index was 17 in the case of Betul while it was 41 in the case of Chhattarpur. Thus, gender equality was more evident in Betul as compared to Chhattarpur.

It is surprising that gender equality in Betul was associated with low economic development. On the other hand, economic development was more pronounced in Chhattarpur. First of all, the proportion of ST/SC population to the total population was as much as 48.3 per cent in Betul as compared to only 27.5 per cent in Chhattarpur. Second, the size of the village was, in general, small in the former as compared to the latter. This is borne out of the fact that the proportion of villages with less than 1,000 population was as much as 79 per cent in Betul as compared to 70 per cent in Chhattarpur. Although the proportion of net area sown to total geographical area and cropping intensity did not differ much between the districts, the development of non-farm sector and banking infrastructure was less pronounced in Betul. As against 15.4 per cent of non-farm workers in Chhattarpur, only 11.75 per cent of the workers in Betul were involved in non-agricultural

Table 4.1: Basic Information of the Selected Districts in Madhya Pradesh

Particulars	*Madhya Pradesh*			
	Reference year	*Betul*	*Chhattarpur*	*State*
Total geographical area (in sq. km)	2001	10,043	8,687	443,446
Total population (in '000)	2001	779	636	60,385
Population density per sq. km	2001	139	170	196
Growth rate (%) of population	1991-2000	31	18	24
Sex ratio (number of females per 1,000 males)	2001	965	869	933
Literacy rate for the entire population	2001	67	53	64
ST/SC population (%) to total population	1991	48.3	27.5	37.8
Male literacy rate	2001	77	66	77
Female literacy rate	2001	56	39	50
Proportion of villages with less than 1,000 population	1991	79.0	70.5	79.1
Normal rainfall (in mms)	2000	1,074	1,083	1,070
Proportion of net sown area to total geographical area in the district	2000	43	41	67
Cropping intensity	2000	119	119	135
Proportion of cultivators to total workers	1991	46.6	62.1	51.4
Proportion of agricultural labourers to total workers	1991	41.7	22.5	34.1
Proportion of non-agricultural workers to total workers	1991	11.7	15.4	14.5
Rural population per rural and semi-urban bank (CBs and RRB)	2001	17,470	15,545	19,211
SGSY groups	2002	3,133	1,852	121,643
NGO formed groups		NA	NA	NA
Swa-Shakthi groups		410	411	NA
Number of SHGs linked to banks under NABARD's programme	2001	10 (2000)	NA	5,699

Note: NA = Not Available

Sources: 1. NABARD, Potential Linked Credit Plans of selected districts.
2. Women Development Corporation, Madhya Pradesh.
3. DCO (1991).

activities. In Chhattarpur, there was one commercial bank/regional rural bank for 15,545 persons. In contrast, each bank in Betul had to cover more than 17,000 population.

Table 4.2: Gender Development Index in Betul and Chhattarpur

Indicator	*Betul*		*Chhattarpur*	
	Male	*Female*	*Male*	*Female*
1. Life expectancy in 1991	52.20	51.70	50.30	44.40
2. Literacy rate in 1991	57.42	33.90	46.87	21.32
3. School enrolment rate (1990)	60.93	49.39	55.74	40.39
4. Worker participation ratio	53.24	39.84	51.65	28.60
5. Share of earned income	0.32	0.68	0.24	0.76
6. Rank within the State	17		41	

Source: GoMP (1998).

Notwithstanding lower development of women in Chhattarpur, the number of SGSY groups formed in the district was less. In 2002, there were 121,643 SGSY groups in Madhya Pradesh State. The total number of SGSY groups in Betul and Chhattarpur were 3,133 and 1,852, respectively. With this background, let us now analyse the key questions raised in the study.

NOTE

1. For an illuminating analysis of efficiency implications of intergovernmental competition, *see*, Bretton (1995).

5

Participation of Members in the Formation and Development of SGSY Groups

Introduction

The main purpose of this chapter is to discuss the participation of people in the study villages, in general, and members of SGSY groups, in particular, in the formation and development of SGSY groups. In general, the phases involved in the formation and development of groups are threefold: pre-formation, formation and post-formation. The studies have shown that the formation of self-help groups is a process, the quality of which plays an important role in the functioning and sustainability of the groups (Rajasekhar 2002a; Satish 2001). Hence, appropriate participatory methodologies are to be adopted to achieve quality in the groups. The studies also note that the quality in the formation of SHGs could not be achieved especially when the responsibility of the formation had been assigned to government departments. Due to factors such as limited staff, inadequate training, target chasing and lack of incentives, the formation process was noted to be *ad hoc*, devoid of quality, and excluded the poor and marginalised. As a result, the groups formed could not survive and many of them became defunct (Rajakutty 1997).

In this context, the following questions arise. What process was followed to disseminate information on SGSY programme before the formation of SHGs? What methodologies were adopted in analysing the situation and identifying the needs of women in these villages? How did the people participate in arriving at decisions on the composition of the group, and formulated rules and regulations on the number of meetings, savings amounts to be contributed, etc.? How did the members participate in the appointment of office-bearers to the groups? What was the participation of members in the meetings, and in the savings and credit programme? How many households managed to undertake new economic activities for poverty alleviation through employment generation? What factors facilitated or hindered the participation of members in the programme? This chapter seeks to answer these questions with the help of data collected from sample SGSY groups and members. Before that, let us understand the meaning of participation and factors enabling and constraining participation by reviewing the existing literature.

Participation

Participation simply means taking part, sharing and being involved. It is a process which concerns the relationships between different stakeholders in a society, such as social groups, community, and institutions at the level of policy and service delivery. It aims at increasing self-determination, and readjusting control of and influence over development initiatives and resources. The World Bank defines participation as a process through which stakeholders influence and share control over development initiatives, decisions and resources that affect them. Participation so defined is not a static input or component but an ongoing and dynamic process (Trond 2001). When linking participation with development, one can say that participation will give awareness and information of the development project, and will make development more precise.

The conventional growth-oriented top-down development strategy has not accomplished the desired trickling down of benefits of development to the marginalised sections. The programmes administered by the outsiders (including the government) view people as objects of development, and that they have to provide services at their command rather than what people need. It is the disillusionment with the failures of the plans and programmes that has sensitised policy makers, administrators and donor agencies to the need for understanding the local realities (Narayanan 2003).

The need for understanding the local realities gave rise to the democratic local governance, which is now a major sub-theme within the context of democratic development. The major premise of new development paradigm is that by building popular participation and accountability into the local governance, the government at the local level will become more responsive to the needs of the people and more effective in service delivery. Another premise is that the democratic local governance includes people from all walks of life in community decision-making (Harry 2000). The main question is that can ordinary people be like agents capable of effecting change? How can the marginalised sections of the society occupying the lowest rung in the hierarchical structure and struggling to derive the livelihood, actualise their dreams of getting some economic independence?

It is in this context that it becomes essential to understand the following: What is the meaning of participation? What are its types? What factors determine the participation in an organisation at the local level?

The concept of participation is multidimensional, ambiguous and broad. The term participation is used differently by different levels of practitioners and it varies with different sets of situations (Uphoff 1989). "Some use the term to mean active participation in political decision-making. For certain activist groups, participation has no meaning unless the people involved have significant control over the decisions concerning the organisation to which they belong. Development economists tend to define participation by the poor in terms of equitable sharing of the benefits of the projects, yet others view participation as an instrument to enhance the efficiency of the projects or the co-production of services."[1] These diverse perspectives truly reflect the differences in the objectives for which the different groups might advocate participation (Paul 1986).

Participation is not a single event. Four main types of participation have been identified, which are distinct from each other though they are interactive and have effects on one another. They are as follows:

1. Participation in decision-making relating to the identification of problem, formulation of an alternative, planning of activities and allocation of resources.
2. Participation in the implementation (in carrying out activities, managing and operating programmes and delivery of services).
3. Individual or collective participation in economic, social, political and other benefits.
4. Participation in the evaluation of the programme and its outcomes which should provide a feedback on (1) to (3).

Following the above, participation is defined as the involvement of people in assessing the situation, identifying the needs, planning, implementation and monitoring of activities. The objectives of participation range from efficiency, cost sharing, effectiveness, capacity building to empowerment. Participation can occur at the initiative of people themselves or development initiating agency. Incentives for participation can vary from remuneration or incentives to coercion. Participation of the people can be either direct or indirect. The duration of participation can vary from *ad hoc* to regular and from intermittent to continuous. Finally, participation can occur at the individual, group and community levels. The purpose of this chapter is to see what type of participation had taken place in the case of SGSY programme? What were the incentives? What were the objectives of participation? Was it intermittent or continuous?

It needs also to be addressed as to what are the determinants of participation? Economists usually apply a rational decision-making model which postulates that all costs and benefits of an action can be attributed with certain values. The rational individual will then weigh up the values of two alternatives and decides to go for that alternative which has a greater value (Weinberger and Jutting 2001). In contrast to this, social scientists usually assume that social behaviour is influenced by factors that may not be explicitly attributed with certain monetary values.

Empirical studies bring out that the following are the determinants of participation. In micro-finance groups, the middle class may be in a more favourable condition to participate in the programme due to its involvement in non-agricultural activities and consequent need for credit (Rajasekhar *et al* 2004). The very wealthy rural households may not participate in such groups due to higher opportunity costs of participation in the meetings, savings contribution, etc. The poor also are unlikely to participate due to higher opportunity costs. Larger number of children in a household (especially school going ones) will enable their mothers to participate in micro-finance groups (Weinberger and Jutting 2001) as grown-up children take care of younger ones or school going children do not hinder their mothers' participation. The social capital stock within a community, measured by the number of organisational networks and groups, will have positive influence on the decision to participate. The expected benefits associated with group membership are regarded higher if a minimum of trust and co-operation within the community exists.

District and Block Level Implementation Arrangement

As noted earlier, at the district level, the Department of Rural Development (DRD) is the key agency to implement the SGSY programme. The CEO is, in general, the officer responsible for the implementation. The day-to-day administration of the programme is, however, undertaken by the Assistant Project Officer (APO). The department undertakes the financing functions of disbursal of funds to the banks towards subsidy, and loans to SGSY groups, and NGOs towards capacity building, as the money earmarked for SGSY is sent directly to the DRDAs.

The programme implementation responsibility has been entrusted to the DRD on the assumption that they could utilise the services of the secretaries of the grama panchayats in the formation and consolidation of groups. As the state government wanted to achieve rapid progress in the programme, it stipulated the targets to be achieved in each district. The target was to form 320 SGSY groups in a block. In achieving this target, the department faced two problems. First, its own officers at the block and sub-block levels were inadequate in number. Second, the grama panchayat secretaries[2] were also insufficient in number. Further, the widespread perception among the staff that they had heavy workload and lacked the required skills in the formation of SHGs, also affected their participation. The department, therefore, felt it necessary to divide the targets among several departments. Consequently, the departments of rural development, women and child development, adult education, agriculture, horticulture and veterinary were assigned the function of formation and consolidation of groups in the selected districts.

In the sample districts, the anganwadi worker, a temporary female staff employed at the village level to take care of the Integrated Child Development Services (ICDS) Centre, was entrusted the key functions relating to the formation and consolidation of the groups. Although anganwadi workers did not have any prior experience in the formation of groups, the department could not provide rigorous training to them due to time constraints. The APO informed that he provided basic knowledge to the block and village level staff on the formation and consolidation of SGSY groups.

Consolidation of the groups was gauged through two-time grading: once to decide the disbursal of revolving credit fund and later the income generating loan. Though the DRD assigned the functions of formation and consolidation of groups to other departments, it took keen interest in these two as the state level monitoring indicators gauged the progress on group formation and monitoring of groups sanctioned with the loan. The gradation process involved the block level officials from the DRD and collaborating department and banks. The DRD followed the progress of gradation in several blocks. The officials at the taluk level noted that they faced constraints as the staff in-charge of the follow-up and consolidation of the groups was inadequate, and did not have adequate provision towards travel. The constraints and difficulties were identified and sought to be resolved at the meeting of the district level co-ordination committee chaired by the collector or CEO. However, delays in grading due to the inability of the banks to participate (given insufficient staff and the vast area that a bank covered) contributed to the inability to solve the problem in the district level co-ordination committees.

The function of monitoring of the programme essentially consists of the compilation of information on the status of the groups. The APO, in charge of the programme at the district level, obtains the information, and helps the collaborating departments in overcoming any obstacles in the formation. According to one key district official, since the state level monitoring indicators were formation of groups and sanctioning of loans, the functions of implementation, external activity co-ordination and conflict resolution received priority. The quality of monitoring was poor at the district level, and focused on quantitative targets.

The function of information dissemination is undertaken by the DRD in the form of distribution of posters, and organising information exchange between line departments and SHGs in the periodic conventions of SHGs at various levels.

Formation of SGSY Groups

Since the SGSY programme rests heavily upon group approach, an understanding of the group formation process in the two districts becomes important to draw any conclusions about the effectiveness of the programme. The process adopted for the community mobilisation, which is central to the group approach, should also be understood. This chapter discusses the findings of the study in relation to the process of formation of groups. Before that, let us present the salient features of the study villages and groups.

The study covered 21 groups in 19 villages in Betul and Chhattarpur districts. The total number of groups was 7 in Betul district; 6 in Ghodadongri and one in Bhainsdehi block. The number of groups studied was 14 in Chhattarpur; three in Rajanagar block, six in Naugaon block and five in Isanagar block.

Table 5.1: Distribution of Households (%) by Wealth Ranking Categories and Sample Villages

District	*Taluk/ Janapad*	*Village*	*Wealth ranking*				
			Very poor	*Poor*	*Middle*	*Wealthy*	*Total (in nos.)*
Betul	Ghodadongri	Dudhawani	42.62	31.15	11.48	14.75	122
		Shobhapur	9.88	62.96	17.28	9.88	81
		Khamaalpur	70.83	5.21	11.46	12.50	96
		Ghodawadi	29.41	35.29	25.00	10.29	68
		Neemdhana	80.56	13.89	5.56	0.00	36
		Chopna	43.04	13.92	12.66	30.38	79
Chhattarpur	Naugaon	Chandoura	60.15	11.28	6.02	22.56	133
		Nayagaon	55.32	9.93	10.64	24.11	141
		Tidni	24.38	52.50	13.75	9.38	160
		Purwa	13.66	42.93	40.98	2.44	205
		Panpura	30.05	31.61	19.69	18.65	193
	Rajnagar	Khajua	18.63	36.51	26.23	18.63	671
		Gora	18.80	47.86	15.38	17.95	117
		Peera	67.30	11.85	8.06	12.80	422
	Ishanagar	Rangua	28.88	25.84	19.45	25.84	329
		Bari	25.48	33.12	33.12	8.28	157
		Khairo	25.38	29.95	18.27	26.40	197
		Nandgaun	29.03	70.97	0.00	0.00	31
		Bardoha	35.05	28.52	21.31	15.12	291
		All villages	34.60	29.70	19.18	16.52	3,529

Source: Poverty mapping conducted in the sample villages.

An attempt was made to categorise the villages, where SGSY groups were formed into three groups (i.e., developed, backward and neither) on the basis of the level of physical and social infrastructure, opportunities for undertaking economic activities and presence of different organisations. As many as 14 out of 19 villages were characterised as backward. These villages lacked basic physical and social infrastructure. For example, approach road was in bad condition or non-existent. The facilities such as drinking water, electricity, etc., were unreliable. The villages did not have the social infrastructure such as school and hospital. The people depended on either wage labour and/or subsistent agricultural production. The marketing facilities for agricultural produce were located at far off places. In general, the production was subsistent lacking market orientation. Four villages could be characterised as neither backward nor developed, where some of the infrastructural facilities were present. Only one village (Khairo) could be classified as developed.

In most of the sample villages in Betul district, the households belonged to scheduled tribes and castes. On the other hand, those in Chhattarpur belonged to backward castes and ST/SC communities. The poverty mapping[3] conducted in each village provided us with a distribution of households by different wealth groups. It may be noted that in almost all the villages the proportion of the very poor and poor was more than 50 per cent. In some of the villages, the proportion was nearly 100 per cent.

Mechanism and process of group formation

The responsibility of forming women's groups under the SGSY programme, as noted earlier, was entrusted to the Department of Women and Child Development (DWCD) and was carried out through its staff members working at the taluk and village levels like the CDPOs and Anganwadi workers.

Most of the groups were formed in 2001. Of the 21 groups, 12 were formed in 2001, 7 were formed in early 2002 and two in 1998. Those formed in 1998 represented the groups formed for other programmes, viz., ICDS and Rajiv Gandhi Jala Grahan Mission, which were subsequently co-opted into SGSY programme. However, this process was not without its own problems. In one case, the process took a lot of time that even after one year of such transformation the group was not completely formed. Secondly, the members in one or two such groups were not even aware that their membership had been changed to SGSY programme now.

All the groups were formed only for women. The people in the two districts were, in general, quite traditional in their attitude towards women[4]. Most of the women were not used to any public participation. Therefore, the anganwadi worker (being a lady) had a great role and responsibility of discussing with the household members, especially with men about agreeing to send the women members to join the SGSY groups. The anganwadi worker at the village level, along with the staff of the ICDS programmes at the taluk level, was actively involved in this work. The anganwadi workers, in any case, had prior association with womenfolk in their villages of work for the purpose of identifying the women and assisting them under the programme of ICDS. They were also familiar with the household members (including men and older women), mainly by virtue of their other responsibilities like immunisation, maternal health and child care, drinking water and sanitation programme etc., all of which had scope for women's involvement and participation. One can, thus, suggest that the choice to entrust the anganwadi worker the responsibility of formation of SGSY groups was appropriate. As Kanti Bai from Chopna told us, "anganwadi worker is from our own village and is familiar with our problems and livelihood means. She is able to identify the needy women to join the groups". This view was supported by many others across the field sites.

In the case of 15 out of 21 sample groups, the anganwadi worker took the lead in the formation process. The participation of anganwadi worker was relatively higher in Chhattarpur district as compared to Betul. This was for the simple reason that in the latter, being a tribal belt and relatively more backward than Chhattarpur, the anganwadi workers were more ignorant of the procedure to form groups. Another reason for lower participation was the dispersal of villages in a wide area that is forest and hilly in nature, thus making it difficult to mobilise participation. It should be, however, noted that the DRD officer at the block level was providing a helping hand to them. The facilitators in the formation of the other groups belonged to the Department of Rural Development and also organisations such as NGOs and youth groups (Table 5.2).

Table 5.2: Facilitators Behind the Formation of SGSY Groups

Facilitators	*Betul*	*Chhattarpur*	*Total*
Anganwadi worker	4	11	15
DRD officials	1	1	2
Youth group	1	0	1
NGOs	1	2	3
Total	7	14	21

Mobilisation of the Community

One would expect that the formation of SGSY groups rested, as per the norms laid down in the design of the programme, upon the process of community mobilisation to prepare the lists of those who qualified for benefiting from the programme[5]. This presupposes that the intended target group was given all the necessary information about benefits of joining the groups. One also expected that the people were given sufficient information and awareness on the process of group formation for achieving the objectives such as participation (attending meetings, contribution of savings, etc.), income generation and poverty alleviation. Thus, as a process, mobilisation involved preparing people to make appropriate and strategic interventions in so far as their livelihood improvement was concerned.

Such a process of social mobilisation requires that the facilitators should be well trained. In the field it was learnt that the parent department just instructed the anganwadi workers to form groups by discussing with women known to her or in the neighbourhood of the Anganwadi centre. But, none of the anganwadi workers had received any formal training or capacity building in their work of identifying members and forming SGSY groups. The procedure to be followed in identifying members to form these groups was not made clear to many facilitators. Most of the Anganwadi workers and ICDS staff expressed ignorance about the goals of SGSY and the rules of group formation.

Nevertheless, the anganwadi workers went ahead conducting meetings in some of the villages. The participants in the meetings differed. In some of the villages, women belonging mainly to the better off attended the meetings. In a few villages, the women attending the meetings belonged to all the categories. In all these cases, the influential men such as village headman, secretary of grama panchayat and so on were present.

As was envisaged in the guidelines, the anganwadi worker did not mobilise support to the programme through an explanation on the objectives, activities and expected impact of the programme. Women attended the meetings and expressed their consent to join in the programme with the hope that they would obtain the benefits. As Kumkum Ben from Bardoha village stated, "we came together mainly expecting a bank loan as soon as possible".

In some of the villages, the anganwadi worker faced stiff resistance from traditional men-folk and even from women in the formation of groups. When they went around the villages in meeting the potential persons and motivating them to join the groups, they were criticised and ridiculed by the elderly men who were not quite used to outside intervention for women. When Tara Bai of Ekta SHG from the backward Khajua village took the trouble of mobilising the local women for enroling them into SGSY groups, men reportedly imposed many restrictions in her work.

Faced with such troubles, some anganwadi workers found it easy and convenient to co-opt the SHGs formed for other programmes into SGSY programme. For instance, an anganwadi worker, who converted a group formed under Rajiv Gandhi Jal Grahan Mission into SGSY group, noted that it was difficult for government staff to form new groups. She noted that "convincing men to permit their wives to join in SGSY programme was difficult because the government staff in the past had promised several benefits and did not keep its promises". The anganwadi workers, hence, actively looked for SHGs formed by NGOs to convert them into SGSY groups and reach the target.

It is not that the anganwadi workers did not make good efforts in all the villages. In some cases, the anganwadi workers played a significant role in informing about the SGSY Programme and convincing women to join for their own good. For instance, Anita

Tiwari, a member, stated that she was not allowed to go outside as she was newly married. The anganwadi worker talked to her in-laws and convinced them to allow her to join the group.

Since group formation procedure was operationalised differently in different villages (personal contacts, calling the people to meetings, taking the help of elite in the village, etc.), it becomes important to analyse the question of who were all included in the group?

Composition of the Groups

The average size of the group formed was with around 11 members. As many as 11 groups had 10 members, while one of them had only nine members. The size of the remaining groups varied from 11 to 13 members. The average size of the group was, thus, small and nonviable. The office-bearers and staff noted that the small size was mainly due to the small size of villages, and the frequent migration that the people were resorting to.

We have worked out the distribution of sample SGSY groups by the share of ST/SC members to total members in a group and Gini ratio on landholdings. These two are expected to shed light on the socio-economic homogeneity of the groups. It may be recalled that, as per the design, the SGSY groups should be formed for those households, which were living below the poverty line.

Table 5.3 shows an interesting pattern in the proportion of ST/SC members to total members in a group. The groups belonged to two extreme cases as far as social composition was concerned. The proportion of the groups having no ST/SC member was exactly one-third. On the other hand, in half of the groups, the proportion of ST/SC members to total was more than 90 per cent. There were distinct inter-district variations in the social homogeneity. While all the groups in Betul had only (or overwhelmingly) ST/SC membership, about 50 per cent of the groups in Chhattarpur did not have even a single member belonging to ST/SC community. Although this could be explained in terms of larger proportion of ST/SC population in Betul, we came across only four villages in Chhattarpur not having ST/SC households. The discussion suggests that while social homogeneity in one way or the other could be achieved, the SGSY groups (especially in Chhattarpur) did not fare well in the inclusion of members belonging to depressed castes. The reason provided by the senior staff of the DWD was that the other programmes meant for women's empowerment like Swa-shakthi scheme, had, in fact, given more space for women from vulnerable background. Hence, when it came to the SGSY programme, membership had to come from those groups that were not SC/ST. Moreover, with the involvement of GP in the formation of groups, there was pressure to include non-SC/STs, 'as households belonging to these castes may not have an opportunity to be included under the other programmes'.

Was there any economic homogeneity in the sample SGSY groups? Gini ratios on landholdings of the members in sample groups have been presented in Table 5.3 to analyse the economic homogeneity. Gini ratio of less than 0.25 indicates near equality, while the ratio of more than 0.5 indicates inequality in terms of landholdings. The information shows that none of the groups fell in the near equality category, while nearly 29 per cent of the groups belonged to extreme inequality category. On the whole, inequality in the distribution of land ownership among members was more pronounced in SGSY groups in Chhattarpur as compared to those in Betul district.

Table 5.3: Characteristics of Sample SGSY Groups

	Betul (N=7)	*Chhattarpur (N=14)*	*Total (N=21)*
Percentage of ST/SC members to total members in a group			
Zero	0	50.0	33.3
<25	0	21.4	14.3
25 – 90	0	0	0
90 – 100	100.0	28.6	52.4
Distribution of SHGs (%) by Gini-ratio on landholding			
<0.25	0.0	0.0	0.0
0.25 – 0.50	14.2	7.1	9.5
0.50 – 0.75	28.6	64.3	52.4
0.75 – 1.00	28.6	28.6	28.6
No information	28.6	0.0	9.5

Thus, although the sample SGSY groups were socially homogenous, they were characterised by inequality or extreme inequality in terms of landholdings of the members. This implies that most of the groups consisted of several landless and a few better-off households in terms of land ownership. How did this happen? This question becomes important given that the mandate says that the groups should be formed for the households living below the poverty line, and the composition of the group should be decided in grama sabha meeting. The qualitative information collected shows that the following were the contributing factors.

- The design of the programme suggests that although the members in SGSY groups should belong to households living below the poverty line, if it was absolutely required, the facilitator could include 30 per cent of the members from the non-poor category of households. It appears that the facilitator had utilised this provision in the guidelines to include the households belonging to non-poor categories.
- The procedure adopted in the formation of groups was least participatory. It took different forms in different villages. While in some of the villages, a meeting was organised, such meetings consisted of husbands of potential members rather than members themselves. A few women belonging to Khajuwa and Nayagaun villages in Chhattarpur noted that they came to know about the programme through their husbands. A few of them stated that they came to know that they indeed had become members of SGSY groups.
- In a few other cases, the anganwadi worker arrived at the selection of the households either independently or in collaboration with influential households in the village. Such influential households were also part of the local elected body.
- In Khamalpur village in Betul district, the group was formed under the leadership of village leaders. In this village, the village leaders informed about the Programme to the people.

- Widespread poverty was also another limiting factor. As Chunni Bai stated, as poor people, they did not have time to understand the 'philosophy' of group formation. Poverty compelled them to concentrate upon earning their livelihoods. Being busy with housework besides working as wage labourers, women found hardly any time to discuss with fellow members about the group. Wage work often took them to places outside their village. Those members belonging to service communities like potters, for example, earned a little extra income by making pots during free time and selling them in nearby villages in exchange for food grains.
- The grama panchayat, which had to be involved in the formation process, was in reality a passive observer of the happenings around it. It was hardly represented in the formation process in a majority of the villages and in identifying suitable women to become members of SGSY groups. No grama sabha was held to select the members for SGSY groups. In some villages, the matter was only referred to the grama panchayat in its regular/scheduled meetings. To a question whether grama panchayat played any role in the formation of the groups, some of the women sarcastically commented that they did not even have the knowledge of how grama panchayat office looked like! SGSY groups were formed by the anganwadi worker and nurtured by her. This gave her the freedom to run the groups as she wished.

What emerges from the above is that the SGSY groups were not formed on the basis of any scientific method relating to group formation. Efforts were not made to assess the situation of poor women and their needs. It is not that the anganwadi worker did not know the condition of the people in the villages in which she has been working for a long time. Then, what were the reasons for the formation of heterogeneous groups in collaboration with village elite and without involving the community in the grama sabha? At least two reasons can be found: first, the formation of groups was viewed as target to be achieved rather than something in which a qualitative process was to be adopted; and second, the anganwadi workers were told that the members in the group should be in a position to contribute regular savings and borrow from the groups. In other words, they were told that the success of a group in the gradation process would depend on the members' ability to contribute savings. At the same time, they were told that most of the members should belong to the households living below the poverty line. This weighed heavily in favour of a few members belonging to better-off category of households and a large number of poorer members. It is for this reason that we found some groups with members having higher capacity to save than others. These groups did not fix uniform savings amount. Members contributed as much as they could. This lead to disparities in savings amounts by different members, and subsequently in the loan amounts. This will be discussed later.

Participation in the Preparation of Rules and Regulations of SGSY Groups

During the formation of SGSY groups, the facilitators are expected to render support to members in a number of areas. An important area is the preparation of rules and regulations governing the behaviour of members in the participation and micro-finance operations of the SGSY group. In general, the rules and regulations are formulated in relation to the following activities and operations of the micro-finance group.

- *Attendance:* Micro-finance groups are characterised by democratic decision-making and self-management. In other words, all the members have to be present in the meeting when decisions are arrived at. The members should also actively participate in the discussions relating to decision-making. In order to ensure regular attendance in the group meetings, the micro-finance groups prepare the rules in such a way that they provide both positive and negative incentives to the members. An example to the rule incorporating positive incentives is linking attendance with credit, while those providing negative incentives are imposition of fines on those members absent in the meetings without prior permission.

- *Meetings* are an important mechanism to enable the members to come together to discuss a number of issues relating to savings and credit as well as non-economic issues. Participation in the meetings is known to be affected by the number of meetings, time and place. In general, four meetings in a month are preferred as they provide an opportunity to the poor to convert the thrift (postponed consumption) into savings. The meetings should be held at a place and time convenient to most of the members in a group.
- *Regular savings* indicate participation of members in the group, and their commitment to the functioning and progress of the groups. Savings also play an important role in the gradation process and establishing linkages with banks as the regularity and amount of savings have considerable weightage in the overall rank obtained by a group, which will, in turn, decide whether the group will receive the finance from the bank or the department. Savings contribution depends on the amount, periodicity and incentives/disincentives. Hence, micro-finance groups prepare the rules relating to the above to ensure regular savings contribution.
- *Credit* is central to a micro-finance group. Since the loanable funds available in a group are insufficient as compared to the needs of members at any point in time, and the equity in the disbursal of loans is an important objective of the micro-finance groups, there is need to prepare the rules relating to the criteria for loan disbursal.

- *Repayment of loans*: Rules and regulations relating to repayment amounts, schedules and replacement are to be prepared to sustain the groups, and to prevent the tendencies of members becoming free-riders.

A micro-finance group can be successful only when it prepares the rule governing the behaviour of members, and ensures compliance to the rules. Compliance with rules will depend, to a large extent, on whether members understand and appreciate such rules. Understanding and appreciation will come only when the members actively participate in the preparation of rules and regulations.

The representatives of 13 out of 19 groups stated that they had rules and regulations, while five of them stated that they did not have any rules. This was in contrast with the statements of staff forming the groups, all of whom stated that the groups had rules and regulations. Evidently, the representatives of five groups did not even know that their groups 'had' rules and regulations.

When the issue of rules and regulations was further probed with the office-bearers stating that they had formulated the rules, it was found that they were only aware of those rules relating to attendance and savings. It was also found that these rules were seldom followed. The discussion with the sample respondents revealed that the facilitator in most of the cases simply produced the list of rules and regulations commonly used in the district, and read them out in the meeting. This implies that the rules and regulations were not thoroughly discussed in the meetings before they were finalised. In fact, some of the women members even expressed ignorance on the goals of SGSY programme let alone the rules and regulations. Many women stated that they were not aware of the programme, and rules and regulations (such as the requirement to save at periodic intervals) when they joined the groups. In the absence of participatory approach to the preparation of rules and regulations, it is not surprising that five of the office-bearers were not even aware that their groups 'had' rules governing the behaviour of members. It is also not surprising that many sample members were either unaware of the rules, or never followed them.

Ignorance about rules of the group did not adversely affect many members. This was due to the fact that they were basically unaware of the importance of group as an organisation to address their livelihood problem and the need to be members. Attendance in meetings, for example, was one such rule about which many women did not bother. In Sandhya Swasahaya Sangh of Panpura in Chhattarpur district, members were confident about receiving all information about the groups' activities from fellow members even if they did not attend the meeting. Lot of faith was vested upon the leader and most of the members did not mind their ignorance about such matters.

Participation in the Appointment of Representatives

The policy formulators suggest SHGs for poverty alleviation and women empowerment as these are supposed to be characterised by democratic decision-making. If SHGs are characterised by democratic decision-making, then the members themselves should elect the representatives. Two issues become relevant in this context.

- In general, each SHG will have two representatives, as the total number of members in each group is small, i.e., around 15. The functions of the representatives are to: (1) call the members for meetings; (2) fix the agenda for the meetings and facilitate the discussion relating to savings, credit, repayment, etc.; (3) resolve the conflicts among members, if any; (4) prepare minutes of the meeting, maintain the accounts and deposit savings in the bank; (5) take social and political issues concerning the members; and (6) establish linkages with banks and government for mobilising the resources for members. Most of these functions can be undertaken by semi-literate and illiterate members. Since the function of maintenance of accounts requires some skills relating to financial management, the practice in most of the groups in India is to have a literate member as one of the representatives, while the other representative can be illiterate. Thus, there is no overriding concern that all the representatives should have special attributes such as literacy, leadership rules, etc. Any member with a little guidance can very well undertake the functions of the representative.

- A representative has to be acceptable to most of the members. This is because the key functions are to do with financial management and conflict resolution. Hence, the representatives should be elected or selected by the members.

Let us now look at the responses of members on who played a role in the appointment of representatives (Table 5.4). The sample members of SGSY groups noted that different actors played large to partial role in the appointment of representatives. Table 5.4 shows that the members played a significant role in the appointment of leaders. However, other actors also played significant to partial role. Nearly 80 per cent of the respondents stated that influential persons outside the group played partial role in the appointment of representatives. Qualitative evidence also supports this. In Chopna village, the representative of the SGSY group happened to be the wife of Grama Panchayat Secretary. Since there is provision to provide subsidy to SGSY groups, persons like secretary to the Grama Panchayat evinced a keen interest in the formation of group as well as in the appointment of representatives with the hope of controlling the benefits, if and when they were obtained. In this group, the wife of Grama Panchayat Secretary has been an active member in attending the meetings and contributing the savings.

As in the case of Khairo, the village leaders appointed the representatives to groups in many cases.

Table 5.4: Role of Different Actors in the Appointment of Representatives (%)

Actors	*To a large extent*	*Partially*	*Not at all*	*Do not know/No response*	*Total (No)*
Members	80.2	8.2	1.4	10.2	147
Influential members	6.1	29.9	51.0	6.8	147
Influential non-members	4.0	79.7	6.8	9.5	147
Line department staff	2.0	21.1	55.8	21.1	147

In some of the cases, the influential members in the group played a partial role in the appointment of representatives. Over 23 per cent of the respondents stated that the staff from the line department played a role. The anganwadi worker, living in the villages for a fairly long time, played a significant role in the formation of groups. Wittingly or unwittingly, she seems to have played a role in the appointment of representatives. In some of the cases, she herself became a representative of the group.

An important role played by the influential members and non-members, and the staff from the line department in the appointment of representatives suggests the following. First, the members elected or selected those persons suggested by the influential persons and the participation of the members was less than desirable. Second, the evidence on appointment of representatives corroborates the earlier finding that members were not involved in the formation of groups. The involvement of ordinary members in key decisions like appointment of representatives was so marginal that members of Goldy Samooh in Tidni village in Chhattarpur did not know who were their president and secretary.

Participation in the Meetings

Meetings are an important mechanism to enable the members to come together periodically to discuss various issues relating to savings and credit. These discussions play an important role in building the self-management and democratic decision-making within SHGs. Let us now look at the evidence on meetings organised and attended by the sample SHG members.

Table 5.5: Conduct and Attendance in the Meetings of Sample SGSY Groups

Percentage	*Distribution of SGSY groups by the proportion of actual to mandated number of meetings in a year*	*Distribution of SGSY groups by the proportion of members attending the meetings*
0	4 (22.2)	4 (22.2)
< 25	2 (11.1)	2 (11.1)
25-50	1 (5.6)	2 (11.1)
50-99	7 (38.9)	6 (33.4)
100	4 (22.2)	4 (22.2)
Total	18 (100.0)	18 (100.0)

Note: Figures in parentheses indicate column-wise percentages.

The SGSY groups, while formulating the rules and regulation, arrived at decisions relating to the total number of meetings, and the time of meeting. The mandated number of meetings varied from as high as four meetings in a month to just one meeting. Three groups decided to hold four meetings in a month, six of them two meetings in a month and nine groups decided to hold regular monthly meetings. However, the evidence on the total number of meetings actually conducted shows that the SGSY groups witnessed varied performance. More than 22 per cent of the groups did not hold any meeting in the last one year as they were already defunct. In the case of 56 per cent of the SGSY groups, the proportion of actual to mandatory meetings was less than 100 per cent. Only in the case of 22.2 per cent of the groups that the meeting actually conducted was exactly the same as the number decided by the groups.

The above shows the hiatus between principles and practice. As the meetings are an important forum for the members to come together to discuss the issues relating to the group, the gap between mandated and actual number of meetings indicates the failure of the staff to support the processes of participation, transparency and accountability. Non-conduct of meetings and less proportion of actual to mandated meetings indicate that members could not even meet regularly. To that extent, the participation of the members in the programme was affected.

The following factors contributed to the irregular meetings:

- Lack of quality in the formation process and inadequate social mobilisation resulted in raising of expectations among the members. Facilitators, in their eagerness to form as many groups as possible to reach the target, promised that a group would become eligible to financial benefits from the Department of Rural Development and the bank only if the members saved regularly for six months. This led to the following responses from the representatives and members. First, the representatives and anganwadi worker[6] did not bother to conduct meetings as per the mandate so long as the members contributed the savings. Second, the members gave low priority to group meetings as they thought what mattered was the regular contribution of savings rather than attendance at meetings. Third, when the benefits did not reach the groups, as was promised, the members lost interest and stopped attending the meetings.
- The meeting time fixed was often convenient to the anganwadi worker. Since she commuted from one village to another, the meeting during the daytime was insisted by her. Thus, the time was inconvenient to poor women depending on wages from agricultural labour and collection of minor forest produçe (tendu leaves) as these women left the homes early in the morning and returned only late in the night. They found that the opportunity cost of lost wage income would be high if they chose to attend the meetings. Added to that they did not find it necessary to attend the meetings as they always had an opportunity to send their savings through neighbours or children.
- Widespread poverty also resulted in non-attendance in

meetings. Members of Ekta group in Khajua village stated that they did not have time to attend meetings. According to them the representatives (being housewives, involved in petty business, etc.) were having free time to attend the meetings. They were confident that those members who attended the meetings would share the information with those who did not attend.

Conclusions

Any intervention on poverty alleviation requires a thorough understanding of the ground reality and processes that generate poverty. In other words, poverty alleviation interventions will have good chances of success if they are designed on the basis of situation and needs of the poor. This implies that SGSY programme should have enlisted the participation of the intended target group not only in the analysis of the situation, but also in the assessment of the needs. The needs cover the formation of groups, composition of the group, formulation of rules and regulations, etc.

The above implies that social mobilisation is an important prerequisite before the groups are formed. The intended target group should be provided with all the information on the programme, objectives, activities and the intended outcomes. The evidence presented in this chapter shows that social mobilisation process suffered due to fixation of target in the formation of groups, inability to train the facilitators, difficult conditions existing in the villages and so on.

Participation of the people was not widespread in the formation of the groups, formulation of rules and regulations, meetings and in savings contributions. In addition to widespread poverty, factors such as systems and procedures adopted in the groups, lack of incentives, inappropriate design and interference from village elite/ influential persons have contributed to limited participation. The limited participation of the people in the programme meant that the performance of the group was affected. Further, this also led to the tendencies of elite capture.

Evidence shows that the proportion of actual to mandated number of meetings was less than 100 per cent in a large number of cases. This means the inability on the part of the facilitators and representatives to hold the meetings as decided by the group. The facilitators from government departments, once the groups were 'formed' to meet the target, did not give much emphasis on the strengthening of groups, as there was inadequate follow-up by higher officials due to problems of limited staff and lack of resources for mobility. The facilitators were also not trained in the consolidation of groups. In addition, the formation process was based on raising of expectations. When the facilitating staff from the government departments could not fulfil the expectations, they did not have the face or courage to meet the members. Attendance in meetings was also affected due to problems of limited livelihood opportunities, inconvenient meeting time, etc.

The chapter concludes that participation meant costs for the poor. The SGSY programme has had limited success in explaining the benefits of the programme to members, and convincing them that benefits would outweigh the costs of participation. The net result was a vicious circle of low participation leading to lower levels of appreciation of the programme, which, in turn, led to either dismally low levels of participation, exit of members from the programme and defunct status of the groups.

NOTES

1. Refers to user organisations combining their resources and management skills with those provided by the government to produce useful services. In so doing, citizen's organisations earn a voice in determining the terms and conditions under which the services are made available, thereby accommodating the preferences and convenience of the users.
2. *Panchayat Raj Update*, Vol. 10 (3), dated March 2003, notes that the position of secretary was lying vacant 'in thousands of grama panchayats'. As a stop-gap arrangement, the state government had entrusted a large number of secretaries with the additional charge of

neighbouring panchayats. This was hampering the routine functioning of panchayats as their meetings were usually postponed because the panchayat secretary often failed to turn up on account of his 'preoccupations in other panchayats'.

3. Poverty mapping was conducted by the field team with assistance from three key informants. In other words, the team facilitated a discussion among key informants to classify the households in the village into several poverty groups. In general, the key informants categorised the households under four groups: very poor, poor, middle and wealthy, and provided the rationale for categorisation. The rationale, in general, was in terms of different levels of deprivation.
4. During fieldwork, it was noticed that women would not talk to male researchers in the absence of their menfolk. Hence, each male researcher had to take a female researcher to introduce him to the women. Often, the representative of the anganwadi centre like the worker or the helper did the role of facilitating such interviews.
5. Mobilisation is a process of creating interest among people about a programme. It is also described as referring to "a significant rise in the degree of popular involvement in the process of societal transformation" (Hettne 1978). A social unit, when gets into a process of mobilisation, gains relatively rapidly in control of resources that were not previously under its control (Etzioni 1968).
6. The anganwadi worker did not call for a meeting during the period of six months even once. Sunder Bai from the Rangua village stated that she did not know the rule relating to conduct of meetings. When asked whether she raised this issue, she said that she did not have time as she was worried about wage labour and declining livelihood opportunities.

6

Participation of Members in Savings Contribution and Credit Utilization

Introduction

Savings contribution and accessing credit facility are two important features of SHGs involved in micro-finance activities. Regular savings indicate participation of members in the group, and their commitment to the functioning and progress of the groups. In the context of SGSY programmes, savings also play an important role in the gradation process and establishing linkages with the banks. This is because the regularity and amount of savings have considerable weightage in the overall rank obtained by a group, which will, in turn, decide whether the group will receive finance from the bank or the department. Savings contribution from the people depends on the following factors: participatory processes adopted in fixing the amount and periodicity of contribution, and secondly, incentives and disincentives incorporated into the programme design.

Credit is central to a micro-finance group. The participation of members in so far as accessing credit is concerned depends on a host of factors; amount available in the group, type of activity chosen, transparency in the selection criteria, responsiveness of leadership, rules and regulations relating to repayment, and repayment itself.

This chapter examines the participation of members in the contribution of savings and availing of credit facility from the groups. It also analyses the factors affecting the participation of members.

Participation in Savings Contribution

Regular savings contribution by the members indicates that the members were taking interest in the micro-finance group, and were keen to contribute to the progress of the group. Savings played the following role in micro-finance groups:

- Rutherford (2000) notes that the poor would like to contribute their savings to meet the needs relating to the lifecycle, emergencies and income generation. SHGs offering convenience (Rajasekhar 2002b) provide an opportunity to contribute savings and meet their different credit needs.
- Micro-finance groups link savings with credit. In other words, the savings of a member should be in certain ratio of the requested loan amount. This implies that unless the members contribute savings they will not be in a position to access the credit facility from the groups.
- Under the NABARD programme on Bank-SHG linkage, the accumulated amount of savings to credit extended by the bank to a SHG will range in the ratios of 1:1 to 1:4 depending on the track record of the group. The level of financial resources accessed from a bank would, therefore, depend on the total amount of accumulated savings in a group. This will make the regular savings to be an absolute requirement for the members to access larger amounts of loans from the groups.

It is, therefore, important to look at the evidence on the amount of savings contributed by the members. Of the 21 groups, three groups did not have any savings as these had become defunct. In the case of other groups, there were savings although the amounts varied significantly among them. The total accumulated amount of savings was less than Rs. 2,000 in the case of 11 groups, while it was between Rs. 2,000 and Rs. 4,000 in the case of five groups. Only in the case of two groups the accumulated amount of savings was more than Rs. 4,500. It should be noted that these two groups had started lending activities, and the amount lent was more than Rs. 10,000.

Table 6.1: Distribution (%) of Members by Total Amount of Accumulated Savings (in Rupees) in SGSY Groups

Savings in Rupees	*Betul*	*Chhattarpur*	*Total*
Zero	7.7	13.7	11.6
0-50	0.0	9.5	6.1
50-100	13.5	12.6	12.9
100-200	57.7	42.1	47.6
200-300	19.2	14.7	16.3
300-400	0.0	7.4	4.8
400-500	1.9	0.0	0.7
Total (nos.)	52	95	147

Consequently, the amount of accumulated savings contributed by each member was small to negligible. Of the 147 sample members of SGSY groups, nearly 12 per cent did not have any savings as many of them belonged to defunct groups. A majority of the members had savings in the range of Rs.100 to 200. This implies that, if savings were linked to credit, a majority of the members could not borrow more than Rs.200 to 400. Small amounts of savings also imply that the savings programme did not help the members to develop confidence to put their savings in the group, and gradually overcome the vulnerability. It is often noted that the growing amount of savings in micro-finance programmes would give confidence to members to undertake income generation activities.

The following contributed to irregular savings contribution by the members:

- The first reason was widespread poverty. Due to infrequent availability of wage employment and low wages, the incomes earned were low. For example, the members of Ekta group noted that all of them belonged to the Potter community. Their livelihood came chiefly from the production and sale of pots in the nearby villages in exchange for food-grains. They did not often get money into their hands to contribute to the savings.

- In some of the villages, the poor often migrated to distant cities and towns, and the neighbouring villages in search of livelihood. Whenever they were out of the village, the savings contribution was affected.
- The procedures adopted in some of the groups did not help in regular savings contribution. Because the groups were heterogeneous, some women contributed higher amounts while others preferred lower amounts. Since savings were linked to credit, the better-off women were in an advantageous position to borrow larger amounts. When the better off did not repay the loan amounts and became defaulters, others lost faith in the group, and they either stopped savings contribution or withdrawn their savings.
- A large number of SGSY groups did not start credit operations either because of smaller amounts of loanable funds in the group or lack of facilitation. The absence of loan facility in the groups existing for more than one year indicates lack of reciprocity to savings contribution. Hence, members stopped the contribution of savings.

Economic Activities Undertaken by SGSY Groups

In so far as income generation through self-employment was concerned, the government did not want SGSY to be like any of the past similar programmes[1]. SGSY was initiated with the aim of assisting the poor households to successfully achieve a stable and better income, reduce poverty and finally, eradicate it in a phased manner. Undertaking of IGA was scheduled to take place under the support and supervision of a three-member committee, including the Sarpanch in each habitation (village). It continues to support the group approach envisaged in the DWCRA programme, where poor families identified for the programme are organised into SHGs and provided with training and capacity building.

The pre-conditions for undertaking IGA are as follows: once the groups are formed, the beneficiaries will identify certain economic activities for purposes of income-generation in collaboration with a three-member committee which includes the Sarpanch. In this process, emphasis is placed on transparency and accountability, the chief characteristics of any decentralised programme. The placing of lists by the Sarpanch before the Grama Sabha for approval is a testimony to the need for transparency in the selection of beneficiaries. Here, besides selection, development and upgradation of skills also take place. This is expected to help in establishing market links. Once these are completed, banks are approached for financial assistance.

SGSY follows the cluster approach for undertaking economic activities. In theory, the programme insists that the selection committee identify four to five important activities suitable to the local situation and to the people who undertake them. These have to be approved by the taluk or Janpad Panchayat and the ZP/DRDA at taluk and district levels respectively. Seventy-five per cent of the total budget comprises of funds for cluster activities. It was expected that the banks and other financial institutions would keep close co-ordination and involvement in the various stages of finalising the project proposals for IGA and in ensuring timely and adequate financial support. This presupposes that the various agencies like the NGOs, CBOs, and the staff of the government and members of the SHGs — all come together and work unitedly to enable the group to establish proper linkages with the banks.

Another significant point is that, once the group completes its six months of existence, it will be 'graded' to assess its status and achievement. Gradation fundamentally assesses the ability of SGSY groups for their built-in capacity to establish linkages with the banks. It is only after emerging successful in such grading tests that the group can claim to be eligible for receiving credit fund that amounts to Rs.25,000. Out of this credit fund, Rs.10,000 is the interest free subsidy from DRDA and Rs.15,000 is the loan from the bank. After another six months, the second gradation is to be undertaken to ascertain the capability of the groups in undertaking IGA through higher level of investment.

The emergence of IGA as a group activity is in itself a significant part of the working of SGSY groups. SGSY programme sought to bring together the various actors responsible for 'identification of income generating activities'. This included processes like identification of people and activities that would go with them and with the local resource situation. Evidently, this is a very strategic decision-making process by the decentralised body. However, the inherent challenge is that it should be undertaken against a democratic background by taking people's consent and consensus. Thus, the scheme encourages democratic decision-making by people both within SGSY groups (for supporting the decisions of the panchayat to undertake certain IGA) as well as outside the group (in the grama sabha). The decentralised bodies are vested with the power to monitor the progress of work and maintain transparency, accountability and participation, the three essential traits of decentralised governance.

How many SGSY beneficiaries undertake new economic activities?

A few SGSY members availed credit from the groups. The amount of loan ranged from Rs.100 to Rs.1,500. However, there were 91 members who had not availed of any such loan. Poor saving habits could be attributed to the poor earnings of members. Instead of calling it their failure to save, one should go by the amount that they were able to save. Besides personal inability to save more, the members were more affected by organisational failures to take off successfully. Almost all groups became defunct six months after their formation, with only the initial deposit of Rs.120 remaining in the account. The groups had met for a maximum of two times before closing down.

Groups in Chhattarpur are better in their savings position. In Betul's case, only one group had accumulated savings of up to Rs.4,500 and that was the maximum. Chhattarpur had members with better savings. Two groups received assistance of Rs.10,000 each here. Betul had one group that received Rs.1,500 as bank loan.

In addition to poor savings base, other factors contributed to the non-receipt of loan facility. Focused discussions with members across field sites have revealed that transparency was lacking in most groups as regards loan dispersal. Most of the members were aware of the rules regarding the above. Meetings were not regularly held. Decisions about who should be given loan were crucial in group's activities. The impressive number of replies that decisions were taken on the basis of general consensus of members should not lead us to conclude that the groups were working well. Women were found to be aware of the fact that they had to save more amount to be able to avail of loan from the group. Hence, many of them refrained from taking petty loans from the group, and preferred to let their savings to accumulate.

Besides the above explanation, another reason for members expressing consensus was that in some villages, members came from homogenous background like the same village, caste and tribe. Thus, they had arrived at an understanding about the perceived need of the applicant for loan. Loan amount, whenever it was taken from one's own account, was not a high amount, but ranged between Rs.200 and Rs.300. It was made clear in focused group discussions that women, who came forward to apply for a certain amount as loan, had made sure that such an amount was available in their account. Therefore, their claims for loan were not found to be objectionable by the fellow members.

But the tragedy of the situation was that while members from poor and very poor background remained content with small amounts of loan, their representatives often with the connivance of either the anganwadi worker or village leaders laid claim to higher amounts. This included two or three cases of those groups, which had made it to avail external loan also. Often, such latter type of members hailed from upper caste/class households and utilised the loan on household assets. Recommendations often came from outside like the TP or ZP, besides, in many cases, the GP also recommended such elite for benefits. Thus, we found that members who had availed of loan were not only relatively better off but also had political weightage.

Under these circumstances, it is not very surprising to find that the programme had limited impact on income earning through employment generation. A majority of the sample SGSY members could not pursue any new income generating activity at all (Table 6.2). As many as 137 out of the 147 members stated that they were pursuing the same activity that they were engaged in before becoming members of SGSY groups. Thus, undertaking of new activities under SGSY was almost non-existent. Ultimately, there was a single case each from Betul and Chhattarpur, where the existing activity had been expanded after the woman became a member of the SGSY group. There were five members who had pursued a different activity. Another three members from Chhattarpur had undertaken expanded or new activity: but with credit from non-SHG sources.

Table 6.2: Distribution of SGSY Members by Activities Undertaken by Them after Joining the Groups

Activity	*District*		*Total*
	Betul	*Chhattarpur*	
Same	49	88	137
Expanded activity	1	1	2
Different activity	2	3	5
Expanded activity with non-SHG	0	1	1
Different activity with non-SHG	0	2	2
Total	52	95	147

An examination of the primary occupation of members reveals the following. From both districts, nearly fifty per cent continued with whatever were their primary occupations, like agricultural and non-agricultural labour for wages. Another 37 per cent of them held cultivation as their primary occupation. Those representing self-employment like in trade and business and in services constituted about 4 per cent.

What contributed to the failure of the programme to enable the members to undertake income-generating activities?

When we go to seek reasons for this type of results, we find that a majority of the villages consisted of very poor or poor households (Table 5.1). The very poor background of members prevented them from mobilising sufficient initial capital to seek external assistance.

The concerned grama panchayat was not in a position to shoulder its mandatory role on collective mobilisation of people and identification of suitable IGA. First of all, the types of villages varied from revenue to hamlets. Betul district has a large number of hamlets due to its hilly terrain and inhabitation by tribals. A large number of villages were also underdeveloped. People failed to take up any IGA due to poor resource condition of the villages.

An important rule followed in many groups was to link savings with credit. Frequent migration of members to far off places in search of livelihood acted as another constraint in attending the group meetings and contributions of savings. Eleven out of 19 villages reported frequent migration of households belonging to lower castes and poorer communities in search of livelihood as they did not have access to land and non-land based livelihood opportunities in their villages. Unable to save regularly, a majority of the members did not have sufficient savings in the group to borrow for income generation.

We find that there was absence of a proper nexus between decentralised bodies and the line departments. The latter had taken an upper hand and the groups were formed by the anganwadi worker not in consultation of the elected representatives in grama sabha. Thus, the absence of devolution of power, knowledge and resources had made SGSY a virtual non-starter.

Adoption of a target-based approach in the formation of groups resulted in less time to consult all the relevant actors. Thus, an organic link between the two had not been thoroughly established. The urgency with which the anganwadi worker was asked to form the groups had led to listing out some names of women only to fulfil the target or to report to higher ups as 'mission completed'. Those responsible for forming groups were themselves not fully aware of their responsibilities and duties.

Under these circumstances, many women members did not know the ultimate purpose of the formation of groups, namely, undertaking self-employment activities for income generation. More than 70 per cent continued to believe that they were in the group only to contribute to savings. Many among them were not aware of the bank linkages for financial assistance.

There were certain checks and balances for the block and district authorities to monitor the progress of SGSY scheme. For example, the BDO at the block level was directly responsible for the selection of key activities, co-ordinating and making arrangements for infrastructure facilities, credit, technology, market and finally scrutinising the block-wise proposals, after consulting the experts. Likewise, the district level officers and representatives were responsible for reviewing SGSY plan, making provision for training, assessing needs of people and reviewing the training arrangements; scrutinising the block-wise proposals after holding consultation with concerned experts – for all these, the district level officers and representatives were held responsible.

SGSY is one programme where linkages play an important role. But with the SHGs and Grama Sabha not playing their roles, linkages are being sidelined. As link institutions, they have failed to carry out their own roles effectively to enable the link institutions to co-ordinate SGSY activities. People's preferences and choices are not heard in the Grama Sabha. Their needs are not linked with the duties of external agencies. The processes of identifying needs and carrying them forward to the concerned people to check the potential for undertaking IGA are totally missing.

Linking selected IGA with markets, which are located nearby, and arranging financial support are crucial. Further, linkages will have to be established with good markets based on the demand factor. Easy and uninterrupted supply of raw material is essential to catch up with the demand for adequate supply. Skill formation and capacity building among group members is yet another issue. The BDO plays a significant part in linking local with block and district level potential. The programme seeks to involve the heads of line departments to achieve convergence of resources to facilitate undertaking of IGA. In most cases, Banks have fulfilled the formality of identifying a suitable IGA in consultation with officials at taluk and district levels, instead of people in a Grama Sabha doing so. The GS has to identify and approve key activities. The bank comes into the picture only later, after the GP has monitored the functioning of groups, key activities identified and approved in the GS. The BDO or CEO approves the list of both beneficiaries and cluster activities. Thus, the GS and GP at the village level, the BDO and the SGSY committee at the block level play the role of establishing needed linkages.

Besides the above, the study has pointed out that there has been no co-ordination, accountability and attempt to succeed. The sample groups failed to reach a level or stage where they could seek credit for IGA. Poverty was the most important constraint for the members to fail in making regular saving habits. Thus, many groups had not reached the stage when they could apply for gradation to access credit. The SGSY Committee that had to work at the GP level either did not exist at all or was dormant.

Thus, despite having the philosophy ideally suited to the context of invisibility of women's work, patriarchal and gender based discrimination in wages and gender specific relations at household and community levels, the objective of enabling women to undertake self-employment activities for income generation has still not been accomplished. The reason can be found in the following:

- IGA was generally looked upon as something different from the main occupation of the household. Women were already involved in the former, as assistants to men. Examples are agriculture, livestock rearing, arts and crafts etc. Thus, whenever the household had to identify an IGA for women who were members of SGSY programme, it looked for the so-called 'feminine' types of activities, such as goat rearing, collection of minor forest produce like tendu leaf, etc. These activities generally received social acceptance as the right occupation for women. They were those, which could be pursued easily given the constraints for mobility for women.

- Activities that guaranteed backward and forward linkages like availability of raw material and marketing outlets were generally preferred to the IGA.
- Illiteracy of a large section of members was another obstruction for undertaking different types of IGA. A little more than ten per cent were literate, without formal schooling. Thus, a majority of the members considered non-conventional occupations as risky and not good to be taken up by illiterate women like themselves.
- Location of villages is an indicator of its development links with the outside world. Many villages had no marketing outlet nearby. Lacking in good and regular transportation facilities, the members from such villages had to end up selling produce from IGA in local shandies, often for a low price.
- Women showed enthusiasm to avail credit from their own savings accounts rather than from a formal and outside agency like the bank. 23 beneficiaries (of whom 16 were from Chhattarpur alone) obtained loan from their own savings. Another 21 beneficiaries stated that there was no need to take loan from the group. Fourteen women felt so only partially. Absence of sufficient savings amount in their account was the reason for 8 cases to decline taking IGA through bank's assistance.
- The silence of a large percentage of our sample itself can be taken as testimony to the fact that IGA had not been started under SGSY.

Despite their inability to arrange for IGA and the required finance for undertaking the same, we found that women were aware of the reasons for the failure of such initiatives. In most cases, women refrained from taking loans from their own savings, fearing that it would reduce their amount of savings. They were aware that a sound saving practice was the passport to bank loan and to IGA.

Conclusions

Limited participation in savings contribution meant that members did not have sufficient savings to borrow for meeting urgent consumption credit needs, and for production. Small amounts of savings also meant that the vulnerability remained the outstanding problem for the poor. The differential amounts of savings contributed by members and savings linked to credit together implied that those having better economic capacity to save were in an advantageous position to borrow from the group and corner the benefits. This also highlights the 'elite capture'.

The analysis on participation of members in credit activities and undertaking of income generation activities shows that the programme had not succeeded in generating viable and locally suitable IGA. In both homogenous and heterogeneous groups, it was the influential groups of households which cornered the benefits. But most often, the loan amount was invested upon already existing economic activities. For those who really thought of starting a new IGA, there were problems of skill acquisition and supply of inputs like raw materials. With absence of linkages between the groups, the GP and the line departments, collective mobilisation of people to identify economic activities was not even attempted.

NOTE

1. Thus, the programme falls in line with earlier programmes like DWCRA, for example, which had adopted similar approach of group formation and undertaking of income generating activities.

7

Establishment of Linkages and Synergy in SGSY Groups

Introduction

The genesis of SGSY has its roots in the realisation that the existing employment generation and poverty alleviation programmes (like IRDP and TRYSEM) had failed in achieving the expected level of success. The perception was that the past poverty-alleviation programmes, be it employment generation or watershed development, had lacked synergy and a holistic approach in achieving their target. They were also not participatory in their nature and did not insist upon involving people in planning and implementation processes. The evaluation studies also referred to the lack of sufficient and suitable linkages and co-ordination between the various actors (line departments, panchayats and NGO). SGSY groups, therefore, were expected to take a proactive role in establishing linkages to take up income generating activities and achieve sustainable development. The line department at the district level and grama panchayat at the lowest level were assigned with functions of co-ordination to harmonise the linkages among several actors. However, the programme placed a lot of responsibility on the groups to implement the programme. The success was expected to reflect the effectiveness of the decentralised atmosphere that is in vogue today. The task was also challenging to the members residing in backward areas and belonging to categories of vulnerable and the poor. They also faced the challenge of taking on the roles and responsibilities many of which were in the domain hitherto of the government departments.

It is, therefore, necessary to answer the following questions based on the findings of the study: What was the procedure prescribed in the SGSY programme to establish linkages and aim at synergy between the various actors? What efforts were made by the groups to get into the process of interacting with the other actors? How did the groups arrive at decision about choosing economic activities? What arrangements were made to ensure supply of raw materials and marketing of produce? How did the groups ensure that all members of the group would participate in IGA and that the selected IGA was suitable to all?

Research suggests that there are two main groups of strategies through which the poor can achieve a change in their condition of poverty. First, there are strategies that are carried out by the poor in an attempt to change their poverty in terms of their resources and assets. Secondly, there are strategies through which the poor or those representing the poor seek to secure their interests by effecting change in the actions and policies of others and, in particular, bringing about change in public policy and in its implementation (Rajasekhar 2004). The latter is important in the present context, since SGSY aims to achieve rural development by bringing about linkages between the various actors in the process.

Thus, an important ideological base of the SGSY programme is the emphasis placed on the fact that poverty alleviation and development in rural areas has to emerge out of the group approach with people's own efforts. At the same time, it is insisted that these groups would indulge in establishing linkages with various other related organisations, like the decentralised bodies, government and Non-governmental agencies, and others.

Theoretical Perspectives on the Role of Linkages in Development

Before we discuss the findings of the study as regards establishing suitable linkages to facilitate the implementation of the SGSY programme, we need to dwell upon the theoretical understanding about what a linkage means in such a programme.

Theoretical arguments in the context of linkages place a lot of emphasis upon their presence in the relations between state and society and describe them as excellent catalysts of development. Literature offers at least two explanations here to sustain this argument: One is that 'complementarity' enables sustainable synergy and development. This again relies much upon the homogeneity of the group concerned. It is further argued that if public agencies are more intimately involved in community affairs, a healthy relationship can be built.

The second theoretical stand refers to the link between synergy and embeddedness. The argument here is that public and private sphere are only assumptions and that the productive informal network enables good development.

Theoretical debates argue that decentralisation is needed for developing countries since the rural and the poor in them live 'face to face' and social norms distinguish outsiders from insiders. Information accounting system and monitoring mechanisms for public bureaucrats are quite weak in these countries. Further, studies have also concluded that the allocated fund does not reach the beneficiaries automatically. Therefore, decentralisation is preferred whenever tastes are heterogeneous. Local government has an information advantage over the upper tier government (Bardhan 2002). But it is generally characterised by resource constraint – material, human and equipment. The local officials perceive local demands but have limited authority to adjust services and citizens' influence at the local level due to lack of linkages and information (Kahkonen and Lanyi 2000). In such cases, the linkages between the community based organisations and grama panchayats work towards the mutual advantage. People's organisations can provide information needed to the elected representatives, represent their interests and secure them. The local elected bodies can undertake the functions of monitoring and convergence of resources through co-ordination.

The effectiveness of decentralisation is considered to be resting upon the design of the system and the institutional arrangements governing its implementation. These channels include voice mechanisms for citizens to express their views to government bodies and exit mechanisms for citizens to switch to non-public service providers. Knowledge about local preferences is necessary for them, whether they use it or not. Thus, organisations among the poor, such as SGSY groups, can be effective voice mechanisms.

Writing about the delivery of services to the poor by decentralised local bodies, Braun and Grote (2002) argue that this becomes successful only under specific conditions. They emphasise upon discovering the channels in which poverty and decentralisation are linked. They play a significant role in making policies influence decentralisation to result in a pro-poor outcome. Information flow is also considered as one among the indices to understand or judge the impact of decentralisation on poverty. Three others are identified, viz., transparency, elite capture and policy cohesion (OECD 2004).

Efficient delivery mechanism by local bodies is highlighted in many other studies. Cornwall (2002), for example, argues in his contribution to the decentralisation and development debate that decision-making about participation is a crucial factor. Aspects of participation like who initiates, who chooses, which method etc., are important to assess the contributing factors to make it effective. This is because enhancing participation by citizens goes beyond mere inviting or inducing people to participate. It should go beyond mere creating spaces to people to express their needs and gather voices. Insisting upon empowerment of local bodies, the studies argue that they have to participate by establishing links with other institutions in order to function effectively.

The role of grama sabha is stressed equally much. It is intended to be the platform for widespread transparency and accountability. Its central function is to take stock of past developments, review expenditure and to decide about new developmental activities in the light of budgetary provisions. It has to assemble periodically to take stock of the situation and to obtain clarification from the representatives on all aspects and activities of the GP. It has to perform this role to obtain development as the result on the expected line (DFiD 2002).

SGSY, constituting one of the largest programmes undertaken by the DRD, at both the state and central levels, relies much upon synergy between various organisations and individuals for achieving its goals. It aims to promote self-employment among women and men of poor households both individually and as members of SHGs. It covers all aspects of self-employment and aims to mobilise the poor through the group approach. It also has a package of facilities like training, credit, technology, infrastructure and marketing. This suggests that it is a process rather than a spontaneous one. Therefore, the facilitative role of a variety of agencies is vital in this context. Besides the various SGSY groups in a village, the others required to participate in this networking could be categorised into two types, viz., those which are mandatory and those which are supportive in nature. The mandatory ones include the line departments, the Grama Panchayat and the NGO, if any. Likewise, the supportive ones include the other groups formed under either Swa-Shakthi programme or the one sponsored by a NGO. The public also forms an important agency in determining flow of funds and benefits whose participation is mainly ensured through the grama sabha.

Composition of SGSY Groups and Structure of Linkages

Learning by past experience, SGSY has been designed to be markedly different from the other employment generation programmes. Thus, the new scheme has not only certain novel features, but also the Panchayat at the district, taluk and village levels implements it. Thus, it depends upon the system of decentralised governance for its implementation. But, at the same time, it has to draw support and assistance from certain other agencies. This presupposes that the two people's organisations, viz., the SHG and panchayat are empowered enough to develop linkages with other relevant actors in the implementation of the programme. Since it is conceived to be not just an employment generation programme but as the one that aims at total rural transformation and development in the long run, it aims to make the beneficiaries self-depending and self-employed persons.

The need for linkages arises during the following phases of implementation:

- The first need is when the groups are formed or in the formation stage.
- The second occasion comes when they need to devise IGA for sustenance, either individually or collectively. This is when the groups would require finance for starting economic activities from formal financial institutions.
- Thirdly, the groups will have to continue to expand their functions thereby achieving sustainability.

Thus, there are various stages in the evolution and working of a SGSY group. The first is group formation. This includes the processes where groups are formed, developed and strengthened to evolve into self-managed people's organisations at the grass-roots level. Then comes group stabilisation through thrift and credit activities among the members and building their group corpus. Here, the groups take up internal lending to the members from the corpus. The last stage is micro credit. The group's corpus is supplemented with the revolving fund sanctioned as cash credit limit by the banks to take up income generating activities. This results ultimately in micro enterprise development, where the group takes up any economic activity of its choice for undertaking income-generation activities.

The potential of micro-finance is clear in many ways. For example, it is hailed as an innovative credit delivery mechanism that ensures viable financial services for the needy. It has the potential to address issues like actualising equitable gains from the development on a sustained basis and can play a vital role in developing nations in fighting poverty.

It is hailed that the micro-finance scene in India is dominated by SHG-bank linkage programme. Though the groups existed even before the linkage programme (under the SGSY and NABARD's

SHG-bank linkage programme), the banks could not recognise their potential as business clients. Thus, they operated independently in most of the cases, each not knowing the strength of the other. Intervening to forge a linkage, besides SGSY, the NABARD has helped in the emergence of a very strong micro-finance movement in the country. The SHG-bank linkage programme was conceived with the objective of supplementary credit delivery services for the un-reached poor, building mutual trust and confidence between the bankers and the poor and encouraging banking activity both on thrift as well as credit and sustaining a simple and formal mechanism of banking with the poor. The linkage programme combines the flexibility, sensitivity and responsiveness of the informal credit system with the technical and administrative capabilities and financial resources of the formal financial sector, which rely heavily on the collective strength of the poor, closeness of effective social mobilisation functions contributing to an overall empowerment process.

There is the precondition that SGSY group has to complete six months of its existence to be able to undergo the gradation process.

Linkages as Per the Design

In the second chapter, we have noted that the grama sabha undertakes the functions of conflict resolution. In addition to this, the list of members and activities has to be placed before the grama sabha for its ratification and approval. The grama panchayat has to implement the activity by forming the groups and consolidating them. It is also supposed to provide the necessary infrastructure for the SGSY members to undertake income-generating activities. SGSY group members have to contribute savings and participate in credit activities. They are also expected to establish linkages with banks to obtain the necessary resources.

The NGOs at the block level are entrusted with the functions of capacity building and monitoring and evaluation. Banks are expected to provide finance, participate in the selection of economic activities and monitor the utilisation of loan for income and employment generation. The department of rural development is entrusted with the functions of implementation, building the capacity with the help of NGOs and co-ordination.

Thus, several institutions are involved in the process of implementation of SGSY. Both the DRDA as well as the elected representatives of the PRIs have to participate in the implementation of SGSY[1], thereby making the process more integrated.

Linkages for Group Formation

In the allocation of functions for the implementation of SGSY programme, the state, the district, the block and the villages are the units or levels, from where the administrative structure and functions are designed and carried out. Going by this definition, the function of forming the SGSY groups is identified with and entrusted to the NGOs at the Taluk level. They are expected to monitor their (groups') progress by providing support, technology, quality inputs and provision of resources. But in reality, it is observed that contrary to what was stipulated in the design of the programme, the NGOs were rarely associated with the task of formation of the groups. The responsibility of forming women's group under the SGSY programme was entrusted to the Department of Women and Child Development. The latter took upon itself the responsibility and entrusted the function further to those of its staff members who were working at the block and village levels.

Role of Line Department/s

The study has shown that there was no linkage established as per the procedure in the formation of the 21 SGSY groups that came under our sample. For example, the procedure insists that all those officials coming under the department of rural development as well as the local elected representatives of PRIs would have to participate in the implementation of SGSY. A lacuna in the programme that came to light through the study refers to the absence of mention of any guidelines regarding the mandated human assets to carry out these functions. The DRDA is delegated to form the groups with the assistance of NGOs wherever they are present. In their absence, (or even when some field sites like Khajuah, Chopna, Ghodadongri etc. had NGO presence in them) the groups are formed directly by the anganwadi worker (hereafter AW), under instructions by the DWCD.

Table 5.2 in Chapter 5 has shown that the maximum number of groups were formed by the AW (Agriculture worker) (9 out of 21), followed by those formed by NGOs (5 out of 21). The members could not remember the AW having consulted anybody amongst them or general public in this mater. Being a grassroots worker, she was nevertheless considered knowledgeable about the poverty level of different households in the village. Yet, she was also expected to follow the rules of group formation that included raising the issue in the grama sabha in its regular meetings or in one called specifically for discussing this issue. Grama Sabha was never called for keeping this specific objective in view. In three villages, the meeting of the Grama Sabha was nevertheless held, but the agenda did not include anything relating to the SGSY programme. In another two villages, the pre-decided lists of women members were sent to the Grama Sabha for a 'formal approval'. While in theory the entire responsibility rested upon the decentralised body at the village level, in practice it was never so. The key nexus should have been between the decentralised bodies taking the support and co-ordination of the centralised units, and government departments. Thus, the idea of bringing together the efforts of different actors (like the panchayat, line department and people) in the process of forming the groups did not really take place.

The AW herself was not knowledgeable about the procedural details of how the groups could be formed. She formed the groups in consultation with her superiors in the government, rather than with local elected representatives and the people's body known as the grama sabha. This suggests that there was poor or no devolution of power, which included even knowledge as power.

Thirdly, the AW had taken the responsibility of forming groups with a target-based approach. The urgency with which she took up this work showed that there was no scope or time for establishing linkages. Official position was used to bring pressure on the people and their households to accept joining groups.

> 'I did not even know that I was a member till about 6 months. The AW used to collect money saying that we would get buffaloes from the government' —Durga Bai, Chopna, Chhattarpur.

The haste in which the AW was asked to form the groups made the formation process without any linkages but only listing out some names of women to be forwarded to higher officials as 'mission completed'.

Some groups like the Shanti Swasahaya Samooh of Chopna and Shakthi Swaṣahaya Samooh of Dudhawani were started only recently (January 2002, i.e., 6 months prior to our study team met the representatives). This has been one major reason offered for being ignorant of the need to form linkages.

But, the members did not find anything wrong in the above procedure, as they were not aware of the correct procedure. Table 7.1 shows that a majority of the members stated that the anganwadi worker undertook the functions of formation, explaining the ways of managing the group, providing books for maintenance, monitoring, etc. According to them, she did well in all these functions. However, a majority of the members stated that the staff did not do very well in the function of co-ordination with the line department. This refers to the inability of the anganwadi worker to obtain funding for the groups.

Interestingly, however, the anganwadi workers did not do very well in organising the meetings with banks for resource mobilisation and training in the selection of income generating activities. Worst was what a large proportion of the members stated that the line department staff did not undertake the functions of providing training on how to establish the linkages with grama panchayats and line departments. Thus, although a large proportion of the members noted that the line department staff undertook the functions relating to formation and did very well in these functions, a majority of them noted that she did not do well in establishing the linkages.

Table 7.1: Functions Undertaken and their Performance in the Functions Undertaken by the Line Department Staff

Functions	*Members (%) Stating that the LD has Undertaken the Function*	*Members (%) Stating that the Performance was Good*
Formation of the LD	90.3	86.5
Explaining on how to manage the group	85.8	70.3
Providing books for accounts maintenance	81.3	74.8
Co-ordination with PIA/line department/NGO	60.6	38.1
Monitoring the LD activities	76.1	61.9
Resolving the conflicts within the group	82.6	65.8
Ensuring that the LD is accountable to the members	77.4	57.4
Training on how to secure benefits for the members	60.0	48.4
Providing capable staff	72.9	63.2
Organising training programmes and exposure visits	70.3	51.6
Explaining how to improve the habit of savings contributions to the SHGs	49.7	41.3
Organising meetings with the banks and government departments to obtain assistance for the members	64.5	44.5
Training on selecting the right income generating activities and making them successful	65.8	38.7
Training on how to establish linkages with GP and line department	54.8	25.6

Did the SGSY groups have linkages with the other line departments such as agriculture, etc? A mapping on organisations and linkages among them showed that only two out of 21 groups had any such linkage.

Role of PRIs

There was the mandatory participation of the GP in the process but it was also not uniform across the field sites. As far as the PRIs were concerned, it was the Executive Officer at the block level who had instructed the senior staff of the Line Department of Women and Child Development and ICDS about the need to form SGSY groups. Discussions with the EOs in the field sites revealed that SGSY is understood or taken by them to be one of the many other governmental programmes for rural employment generation and development. The concept of empowering the group to progress in its work in a phased manner was non-existent. This included identification of suitable women as beneficiaries, giving them knowledge about the procedure and preparing them to take up any IGA, after establishing contacts with the bank, panchayat and other institutions. Whatever rules existed were actually framed by the facilitator (AW). Moreover, they varied from group to group irrespective of whether they were concerning the frequency of meetings or the amount of savings.

The panchayat, on its part, was also found to be ignorant about the need to develop contacts with other institutions in promoting these groups. Despite variations in its role across field sites in implementing the programme, the GP had not taken a proactive role from the beginning in finding a suitable IGA for each group (Table 7.2). As a grassroots organisation, it was expected to have a reasonably good knowledge about the availability of raw materials for engaging in certain economic activities. But in reality, the groups suffered a long period of inactivity ranging from four to six months since their coming into existence.

Establishment of linkages with other organisations was affected also due to the composition of groups. Both Chhattarpur and Betul had reported cases where women from poor and landless households had not evinced any interest in attending the meetings and in making regular contribution to savings. Migration being a regular practice among most of them, the functioning of the group was continuously getting affected.

Table 7.2: Statements of Presidents of Grama Panchayats on Their Functions in Relation to SGSY Groups and How Well They Have Performed the Functions

Functions	*Statements of GP Presidents (%) on*	
	Undertaking of functions	*Performance of functions*
Co-ordination between line department and SHGs in sectoral activities	90.9	63.6
Supervising the anganwadi worker	72.7	45.5
Feedback to TP/ZP on the functioning of the staff of LD	72.7	63.6
Mobilising funds from the Banks for undertaking sectoral activities	54.5	10.4
Assisting SHGs to obtain local support and co-operation	45.5	27.3
Ensuring that SHGs undertake their activities	63.6	18.2
Providing LD/GP staff to build the capacity of SHG members	18.2	9.10
Providing material assets for the development works of SHGs	18.2	9.10
Providing the GP staff for helping SHGs in undertaking sectoral activities	27.3	18.2
Providing funding support (grants, etc.) to the SHGs to undertake sectoral activities	27.3	9.10

Source: Questionnaire for GP Presidents.

Monitoring of groups' working and providing enabling mechanisms for them to function are functions of the GP. Of specific importance is the period between formation of the group till some income generating activity is identified. Grama Sabha is an institution that has the responsibility of taking decision about the type of IGA and approve the decision of the groups about selection of beneficiaries to undertake such economic activities.

Likewise, the GP has not fared any better in its relation with the higher-level bodies like the Block (Janpad) Panchayat and the district Panchayat. What is important to note is that the GP was delivering its mandatory functions among which implementation of such programmes like SGSY was viewed as nothing but 'a routine bureaucratic function' of the line department, rather than comprising one demanding participation by the panchayat as a people's organisation.

Linkages for Consolidation

Identification of suitable economic activities and selection of members of SGSY groups (as beneficiaries of bank loan) was the next area for synergetic relations in the programme. In fact, this included considerable effort at community mobilisation also to create interest among the members to undertake IGA. In other words, there were two challenges here before the implementing agency. They were: (a) providing awareness about SGSY that it did not mean only the formation of groups for savings activities. This was the general impression with which the self-help groups formed earlier had worked, and soon became defunct. (b) the second was to mobilise support from the GP and various line departments for mooting IGA and establish sustainable backward and forward linkages. Both called for extensive use of the skills of the group to establish suitable links and bring about synergy in action and results.

It is argued in literature that endowment played a crucial role in synergetic relations, i.e. in both leading to such a relationship and in sustainable functioning. Therefore, the study looked into endowments in terms of assets – human, material and financial – of the groups in trying to establish suitable links with relevant institutions.

Human Resources

Human resources in the implementation of the programme comprised the members and their representatives, staff of the line department and of the GP. Establishment of linkages with concerned institutions and individuals for all the three stages of functioning of the groups (and therefore, the programme) rested obviously upon the quality and numerical strength of the group.

The study has found that the groups faced a number of handicaps and problems in (a) possessing the required type and number of human resources; and (b) in building their capacity to perform in the required roles. The study has come up with the following reasons for such a situation.

As noted already, SGSY believes in the process of social mobilisation earmarking considerable preparatory time for the groups to be formed. It is designed to achieve people's participation. But due to bureaucratic hassles and 'target-achievement' type of approach followed by the DWCD, the groups were formed in haste, i.e. when it was a dire necessity to report progress. In the maximum number of cases, it was the AW who was chosen to identify women as members. This was so since as the grassroots worker she was considered knowledgeable about who really constituted the category of the poor in the village. The study points out that having her own problems relating to work load and lacking in infrastructure and resources at her disposal, she resorted to identifying those who (a) were known to her; or (b) those who were recommended by the GP or by her superiors. Power politics being what it is in rural areas, decentralisation of governance seems to have made little or no breakthrough into the hegemony of caste and dominance-based decision-making in selecting beneficiaries for development programmes. Table 5.2 presented in Chapter 5 has noted that a maximum number of groups was formed by AW followed by other organisations (NGOs). There were a few groups formed under ICDS but converted as SGSY ones.

Irrespective of who formed them, the groups possessed largely illiterate members. They were generally from landless background and depended upon wage work for sustenance. The villages in both districts from where these women hailed were either underdeveloped or semi-developed, the last being true of few villages only. Thus, the women were ignorant of the procedure and objectives of the programme. They were found to be lacking in awareness about the need to undertake IGA. The common knowledge was that they would receive loan from the government. This was the incentive offered for agreeing to join the group.

The AW on her part was also ignorant of the objectives of SGSY in most cases. Except in few villages like Khajuah and Neemdhana, a large majority of them mentioned that they only followed the instructions of their superiors and formed the groups by including names of their own kith and kin and a few acquaintances to enable representation of caste and class groups. The AW failed to come up with any convincing answers about her knowledge of procedures and rules. She was not trained in the task of group formation and in transferring skills and in building capacities of the group.

> Even being an official (as 'helper' in the Anganwadi centre) has not enabled me to learn about the need to have linkages with other organisations. —*Ratna Bai from Chopna*

There is participation nonetheless by the panchayat at the block level in many cases. This is clear when we find many groups being formed by the EO at the block level, through the staff of DWCD. In Dadhudhana of Betul and in Peera of Chhattarpur, absence of linkages is attributed to the fact that the village leaders nominated the representatives of the group.

The link between the groups and the sponsors (EO, AW etc.) ceased to exist once the groups were formed. There was no communication and sufficient information about what was to be done after this stage. Illiteracy and social restrictions on their mobility prevented members in many cases to question the former about the procedure.

The GP in most cases comprised representatives and members who too were illiterate and unaware of their rights and liabilities. Often, the BDO took the initiative to suggest names sitting at his block office. Politicians in the ranks of MLAs and MPs influenced decisions favouring their own vote bank. Grama Sabhas were not held in many cases, and even where they were held they went unnoticed by many people, both members and non-members.

Thus, there was no organic linkage between the panchayat institutions, line departments and the groups. This could be attributed not to the unpreparedness of human resource, and to its quality. The ideals of SGSY present in its ideals were not opened up for the people to see and realise its merits and what was new in it. Thus, whoever joined the group was lured by the attraction of 'loan'.

Therefore, we can conclude that the available human resource as an endowment was of poor quality in building the groups to reach their goals. Thus, none of these people was trained in the task of various stages of implementation like group formation, undertaking of IGA, skill formation etc. Being ignorant of the activities to be taken up, rotation of leadership and such other organisational matters, the groups failed in establishing the needed linkages with others.

Besides lack of actual establishment of linkages, lack of knowledge about the need to develop linkages with one another created many operational problems to the groups. This resulted in the groups functioning as disjointed units with no links with the other local organisations. By functioning, they tended to infer that they had to keep meeting and contribute to savings. Such knowledge was also limited to the office-bearers and in most cases had not percolated down to the members. Therefore, the initiative to undertake IGA suffered in most of them.

Deepika SHG is a typical example of how the local power structure curtailed the expansion of economic activity by the group. One of its members, Lalita Devi, a SC, had received land of 2 acres from the government sometime in 1998. Since it was not an irrigated land, the family did not cultivate it but were using it for grazing. But once she became the president of Deepika SHG she offered to use the land for starting a goat rearing activity by the group. It was not a problem, considering that the group was homogenous with all members being from the same caste and were even relatives. But the GP did not agree for the proposal and did not take initiative to link the group with the bank for financial assistance. Once she joined the group, her land was captured by the dominant castes that were her employers for wage work. The family was afraid of claiming land, fearing beatings from the village elders.

The GP on its part also remained silent on the issue of linkages. Basically, there was no difference between the groups and the GP as far as knowledge about the need to take initiatives was concerned. This related to the contact between the staff of government and the financial institutions (the banks) to discuss the feasibility of undertaking economic activities and such other issues.

Intra-Group Relations

The groups also suffered from indiscipline in their functions, like regularity in participation, etc. This is crucial for building up a rich human resource potential in any group. For example, there were no rules at all in 8 of the 21 groups about rotation of leadership. They were unaware that there ought to be some rotation.

In most cases, there was no transparency in the decisions taken. Office-bearers made all the decisions in many cases, while in others it was the representative of NGO who took such decisions.

Thus, the human resource at the disposal of each group under the programme was very poorly equipped with the necessary knowledge, skills and capacity to enable linkages to take place.

Material Resources

Absence of synergy also affected another important area, i.e., the accumulation of material endowments by the SGSY groups. Such endowments are generally of two kinds: (a) the savings of the group over a period of time that would reach a certain amount; and (b) those economic assets of the group that are obtained through the local GP and used as support or base for undertaking income generating activities either collectively or individually.

> Awareness about representing our problems with the Panchayat and the right to take credit from financial institutions like banks are lacking. We did not think about forming any alliances.
>
> —Champa Bai, Dhudhavani, Betul

But there were also instances where some representatives used their official position to gain benefits under SGSY scheme. Rashmi Avasti, AW from Dudhawani, used the group for her own benefit. She was aware of the details of the scheme since her husband was working in the local panchayat. Being the treasurer of her group, she saw to it that the Grama Sabha was held to finalise the proposal to initiate development works in the village, with the permission of the GP.

Savings of the groups

As discussed already in the previous chapter on participation, we find that the financial condition of a majority of the groups was deplorable, and it was difficulty to enable them to invest it to undertake IGA. The groups comprised mostly the poor and landless women who depended upon wage employment both locally and outside for survival. This affected their ability to make contributions to savings and increase the total economic base of their group. Distress migration made many members become irregular in attending meetings and to save regularly. Many groups were left with only the first or at the most the second time contribution leading to a total saving of less than Rs.1,200 per member. In many cases, there was no second meeting at all.

Asset formation

Lack of suitable material assets caused by poor savings is compounded by another factor, viz., lack of any material support from outside. The groups being in such a position to take or not to undertake any IGA on their own also is responsible for the absence, or presence, of poor linkages. The material assets of the group comprised land, livestock or other resources that would enable undertaking suitable IGA by the members either collectively or individually. The members of the GP considered the SGSY groups as government groups, meaning those that were formed to fulfil the target for a scheme. Thus, the representatives had not been taught to, or trained in, establishing contacts with the GP and the bureaucracy to receive benefits/assets that would facilitate undertaking IGA.

Women from Sarayu SHG in Betul told us that they had not seen how a GP office looked. They depended upon wages earned from the collection of tendu leaves as MFP (Minor Forest Produce), which was sold in the local Shandies. Moreover, they were afraid of asking for more details, fearing scolding from the village elders, upon whom they had to fall back during crises situations. Thus, the members expressed lack of time to go round and make contacts with other institutions and individuals, to be the reason for poor linkages.

Thus, in the material endowments too, the absence of synergy is glaring. Except in about two cases, none of the groups received external assistance. The local panchayat is not empowered to take the initiative and involve itself because of the role of the staff of DRD.

Financial Resources

It has been found that the major problem in the context of synergy or establishing linkage between the various actors in the implementation of the programmes lies in defective programme guidelines. Although banks and other promotional agencies are expected to participate in implementation, there is nothing binding upon them to do so. The programme envisages an effective devolution of power and funds. The beneficiaries are encouraged to participate in their own self-development through certain incentives and disincentives.

Under normal circumstances, the groups have to consult the local financial institutions like the banks for assistance. However, the rule stipulates that the groups have to undergo a procedure called as 'grading' to qualify for the same. Knowledge about the scope for suitable initiatives that would link their need to a pre-existing institutional help was found lacking among most of the groups. Table 5.1 on poverty category of households in the sample presented in chapter 5 shows that nearly 50 per cent of the sample households were from very poor category. Thus, poverty (which is a complex blend of landlessness, low caste status and resultant vulnerability) emerged as the main cause of absence of material assets. Besides poverty, taboo on women's participation in the public also acted as a further deterrent. Table 5.1 clearly shows that more than 50 per cent of the groups belonged to very poor category. A large majority of them were from ST/SC background (see Table 5.3). With household income being low and uncertain, nearly 20 per cent in Betul and 4 per cent in Chhattarpur never attended meetings. Rules were imposed on members by less than 50 per cent of the groups, but the severity was missing. For example, members received interest on their savings. Defaulters were seldom fined in 11 out of 21 groups. Even though the rule that contributions would have to be linked to benefit/savings to credit existed; it was often never followed (in 7 or 8 out of 21 groups). About three groups had no rules existing in this regard. For less than 25 per cent, participation in meetings was occasional. Another 30 per cent had no rules and regulations of their own. Extreme backwardness of the group resulted in its weak bargaining power depending upon external agencies to arrange for resources. There were no training activities for most of them. Those, which underwent some such training, had not benefited much since the training did not match with the availability of raw materials locally.

Thus, neither the group approached the GP or LD for skill development nor the latter took up initiatives on their own to establish linkages.

The process of establishment of linkages both between people's organisations and between them and the government agencies suffered due to the failure of the decentralised system also. People continued to see even the panchayat as part of the bureaucracy or itself being the bureaucratic structure. The problem was linked to a situation where guidelines 'about what needs to be done', were absent. The banks and other 'promotional' agencies were expected to participate in implementation of the programme. But there was nothing binding upon them to do so. Devolution of power and funds were prerequisites for its success.

Synergy is lacking in yet another way. It was stipulated that SHGs formed under earlier programmes like DWCRA, Swa-shakthi and those formed by NGOs etc., should have been strengthened to establish synergy between them and the SGSY groups. Focused group discussions have shown that the SGSY groups did not have any form of contact with their counterparts initiated under Swa-Shakthi programme and those formed by the NGOs.

Linkages and Gradation

What was worse, in many cases, the process of group formation itself was incomplete even after two years after the process had started. The programme was introduced in 1999-2000 while the groups were incomplete in their membership even by September 2002 when the study was made. Being still in their formative stage, and not completed 6 months of their existence, they were disqualified from the process of gradation.

Gradation is a stage where the groups graduate from being mere savings-oriented ones and begin to involve in income generating activities. In fact, this is the testing time for progress achieved hitherto in forming the group and in establishing linkages with outside agencies for financial assistance in the main and for other support. The banks and NABARD, given their uncompromising nature regarding the eligibility norms applied to select beneficiaries, would resort to action (of sanctioning loans) only when the project proposals are prepared as per the regulations.

It is felt that it is still premature to expect the decentralised bodies to undertake the task of establishing linkages with banks and other organisations on behalf of the SGSY groups. The reason is that the Panchayats themselves are still not established institutions, so as to be able to achieve complete devolution of power from the state and from other agencies. The GP, in particular, is still a weak institution in the field sites, lacking in adequate human and material resources. Secondly, presence of other programmes, which also encourage groups to be formed, like the

Swa-Shakthi project, has, in fact, weakened the position of SGSY groups (interview with the President of ZP, Chhattarpur). Unlike the former, they are devoid of any NGO support.

For example, in Chhattarpur's Peera village, the Swa-Shakthi group formed by the NGO is working well. According to Rekha Bai, the SGSY group, on the contrary, works only on paper. The group does not have anybody to give it guidance or awareness.

Lack of accountability as a determinant of synergy is important too. Regular interaction with swarojgaris by various officials and panchayat members are absent. Transparency in the selection process with the grama sabha as the testing ground is also absent. Thus, synergy of interests and action is non-existent. Even when it exists, it has not blended well to lead to the establishment of suitable linkages.

But the representatives of GP in many villages have expressed ignorance about the details of SGSY programme. The district administration claims that the programme is successful. Besides all these, the absence of a participatory approach to group formation and grading and the exercise of bureaucratic control over the entire implementation procedure, have sidelined the decentralised bodies and made linkages still a farsighted dream.

Summing Up

Thus, we find that there is considerable bureaucratic control upon the entire implementation process adopted in the case of SGSY. Although theory places heavy emphasis upon state and society linkages as being excellent catalyst for development, and despite the programme envisaging it in principle, it has not yet been successfully achieved. Complementarity is expected to enhance sustainable synergy and development. However, the field data do not prove all this. First of all, it appears to be premature to expect the decentralised bodies to undertake the task of establishing linkages with banks and other institutions. The PRIs themselves are not yet established firmly and independently as democratic bodies with power suitably devolved. The functioning of the groups is not transparent. This has resulted in criticism and led to suspicions about their accountability. Although SGSY is open to all, our sample consists of only women's groups. In a way, this has shed light on certain special challenges for women's groups, given their illiteracy, restrictions on mobility and feminisation of poverty.

NOTE

1. However, the guidelines of the SGSY programmes do not mention about the required human resource or assets to carry out the above functions.

8

Conclusions

Decentralisation is a process that transfers significant political, administrative and fiscal responsibilities to local elected bodies, community based organisations, NGOs, etc., and the empowerment of the communities to exert control over these local bodies. The decentralisation efforts in India aim to bring the government close to the people so that information asymmetry in capturing the situation and needs of the people is minimised, and appropriate programmes are formulated and implemented. There are, thus, close links between decentralisation and poverty alleviation. Policy makers are often confronted with the following questions before a programme is formulated. Who are the poor? Why are they poor? What is to be done to alleviate poverty? It is believed that decentralisation, by bringing the policy makers and programme implementers closer to the people, will help them to find answers to these questions in cost effective manner. Decentralisation, also helps in the preparation of need-based plans, effective implementation of programmes and monitoring them in participatory manner. This also leads to mobilisation of resources – both human and financial.

Although the proportion of population living below the poverty line in India declined, such a decline has not been uniform across the regions and social groups. In particular, women seem to be suffering from disproportionate burden of poverty. Further, the problem of poverty seems to have entered into a new dynamic and complex process. This calls for a specific set of policies to prevent the non-poor falling into poverty in addition to those aimed at poverty alleviation.

Poverty in India has a strong gender dimension. In order to develop and empower women, the government has been formulating policies and programmes, which have been operationalised through five-year plans since independence. A review of the policies and programmes is undertaken during and at the end of each plan period while preparing plan documents. Such a constant review, based on evaluation and studies conducted on government-initiated women development and empowerment programmes, and the successful 'programmes' of civil society organisations within and outside the country, together with political mobilisation of women, have resulted in the following changes:

- A shift in policy focus from 'welfare' to 'development' and to 'empowerment' during the Five-Year Plan periods, especially after the 1970s.
- Assignment of functions relating to women's development and empowerment to different types of local organisations, line departments, local government, NGOs and others.
- Mandatory representation of women in the decentralised government at the district and below.
- Formation of grassroots level women's organisations for their development and empowerment.
- A shift in targeting strategy from 'individual beneficiaries' to 'Self-Help Groups (SHGs) of women involved in micro-finance'.
- A shift in strategy from issuing loans to individual beneficiaries to using micro-finance as an instrument for development and empowerment of women organised in SHGs.

All these indicate that good governance principles have been sought to be applied to women development and empowerment programme. SGSY programme seems to reflect the global thinking and also the views of Indian government on 'good governance'. The term has been defined as an instrument that will help overcome the challenges of poverty and deprivation.

For the Government of India, governance means "the management of such processes that, in any society, define the environment which permits and enables the individual to raise his/her capability levels, on the one hand, and provide opportunities to realise his/her potential and enlarge the set of available choices (GoI 2002b), on the other. The policy formulators have seen a close relationship between good governance and the success of poverty alleviation efforts. The government identified the following as key factors which adversely affect the process of implementation of rural development programmes:

- Excessive compartmentalisation of executive into ministry/ departments.
- A narrow sectoral approach to conceiving, formulating and implementing schemes.
- Prevention of mutual synergies that are inherent in most social sector programmes to benefit the plan initiatives.

Large-scale leakages and the consequent continuation of poverty and deprivation are identified as the fallout of the poor governance of the rural development programmes. The government identified the following strategies, as part of its good governance agenda to improve the functioning of the poverty alleviation programmes:

1. Ensuring participation of the people at all stages of programme implementation.
2. Decentralisation of planning through involvement of Panchayat Raj institutions.
3. Involvement of voluntary organisations, NGOs to supplement and complement the efforts of the government.
4. Formulation of developmental programmes in a more systematic and professional manner.
5. Right to information.
6. Empowerment of the marginalised and excluded sections of society.

Shylendra (2004) concludes that the new good governance paradigm suggests pluralisation of state for development. Development challenges are to be addressed collaboratively by partnerships among the State, market and civil society. The linkages and relations among different actors are to be harmonised through capacity building and co-ordination.

Guided by the new thinking on 'good governance', the policy makers emphasize that SGSY programme is different from all the earlier programmes. SGSY seeks to enable the people to participate in the programme. This programme, being implemented by the central government all over India since 1999, aims to promote self-employment among women and men, and enable them to cross the poverty line. The programme seeks to organise the rural poor into self-help groups through the process of social mobilisation. The SHGs are expected to mobilise savings, have linkages with banks, Panchayat Raj institutions and line departments and collectively decide the economic programmes to be taken by the members. The SGSY emphasises asset building, employment and income generation among the poor; but with a difference. Community orientation of a programme, group-based approach, implementation and monitoring by grama panchayats are its chief and unique traits. The programme seeks to initiate the processes such as participation, accountability and transparency for successful implementation.

The SGSY programme aims to establish close linkages with decentralised institutions, and achieve the development outcomes through good governance principles of participation, transparency, accountability and linkages. In this context, the following questions become relevant. What have been the processes followed in the programme implementation? Did the programme succeed in mobilising the people in the formation of SGSY groups, and in planning and implementation? What was the participation of the people in savings contribution, and borrowing from the groups? What were the linkages between the groups formed under the programme, on the one hand, and decentralised government, banks, etc., on the other? Was right kind of synergy and harmony among multiple players generated?

Since the programme was implemented only from 1999 onwards, it may be too early to analyse the impact of the programme in terms of employment generation, asset creation and income increase. Nevertheless, one question that can be asked is: Is the programme on track in so far as achieving the objectives of enabling the poor to undertake self-employment activities for poverty reduction?

Objectives of the Study

These questions become important given that this is an all India programme with huge budgetary allocation (Chapter 2). It is in this context that this study sought to address the following objectives in relation to two districts (Betul and Chhattarpur) in Madhya Pradesh. Against the backdrop of decentralisation reforms in Madhya Pradesh, and the relative backward status of the state, it would be interesting to analyse the extent to which decentralisation and good governance contributes to poverty alleviatiosn through employment generation. The objectives of the study were to examine:

- what processes were followed in the formation and consolidation of groups?
- what was the participation of people in savings contribution and borrowing from the groups?
- what were the linkages between SGSY groups, and banks and grama panchayats? and
- was the programme on track in so far as achieving the objectives of enabling the poor to undertake self-employment for poverty alleviation?

Methodology and Data Sources

The primary data were extracted from the database built for the World Bank project on Roles of Rural Local Organisations in Development Projects. The household data used in this study pertained to 19 SGSY groups located in Betul and Chhattarpur districts of Madhya Pradesh. In addition, data were also collected from the representatives of SGSY groups, grama panchayats and staff of line department. A separate visit was undertaken to the study districts to collect additional secondary data, and to conduct interviews with key stakeholders such as District Collector, Chief Executive Officer and block development officer. Further, qualitative information from the groups was also collected.

In all, data were collected from 147 households having membership in SGSY groups. The households were randomly selected after obtaining a list of members in the SGSY group. The study also came across defunct SGSY groups. Even in these cases, data from members of defunct groups were collected to identify the factors contributing to the failure of SGSY programme.

Betul and Chhattarpur are vastly different in their location and historical legacy. Betul is located on the southern boarder of the State and has Maratha culture. On the other hand, Chhattarpur is located in the Bundelkhand region, bordering Uttar Pradesh in the north-eastern side.

In terms of total geographical area and population size, Betul is larger than Chhattarpur. In terms of women development, the indicators show that gender equality was more evident in Betul as compared to Chhattarpur. But gender equality in Betul was associated with low economic development. Notwithstanding lower development of women in Chhattarpur, the number of SGSY groups formed in the district was less. In 2002, there were 121,643 SGSY groups in Madhya Pradesh State. The total number of SGSY groups in Betul and Chhattarpur were 3,133 and 1,852, respectively.

SGSY Programme: Progress at the Macro Level

An analysis of trends in the performance of SGSY was carried out with the help of data collected from the Ministry of Rural Development, New Delhi, for the five-year period of 1999-2000 to 2003-04. The indicators such as allocations and utilisation of funds earmarked for the programme, purpose-wise distribution of the financial resources and availability of credit facility to swarojgaris were looked at to analyse the financial progress of the programme. In order to do this, the aspects covered were the progress in the formation and gradation of SGSY groups, number of swarojgaris assisted and coverage of swarojgaris belonging to disadvantaged and vulnerable groups. The key findings are as follows:

The quantum of funds allocated for SGSY programme have, in general, declined. The proportion of releases by the central and state governments was, however, nowhere close to 100 per cent during the entire five-year period. This suggests the capacity related problems among rural development agencies in the utilisation of allocated amounts and/or problems in the disbursal of allocated amounts.

The amount utilised by the programme was generally higher than the allocated amount during the five-year period largely due to high opening balance amount. The proportion of funds utilised to the available funds for the programme generally improved; but, never close to 100 per cent. The shortfall in the expenditure was mainly on account of less expenditure on infrastructure development and skill related training. Although the programme envisaged infrastructure development and skill provision before income generating activities were promoted among swarojgaris, the budget utilisation shows that this was not the case. An obvious implication of this was that the credit for income generating activities to swarojgaris was provided without the necessary infrastructure and social mobilisation of the poor.

The gradation criteria adopted in the programme aimed to ensure that a group passed the grades I and II only when it was strong in self-management and credit discipline. Since the groups passing through the grades were eligible to obtain credit, the trends in credit mobilised by swarojgaris provided an indication on whether the programme succeeded in forming strong SHGs, inculcation of savings habit and incorporating credit discipline. The proportion of achievement to the targets on credit mobilisation was, however, well below 100 per cent. Further, an improvement in the achievement was more because of reduction in the target rather than credit mobilised by swarojgaris. Lower proportion of subsidy disbursed to SHGs (as compared to that provided to individual swarojgaris) leads to two suggestions. First, since the subsidy disbursed was in proportion to the credit mobilised by swarojgaris, the implication was that the programme was focusing on individual swarojgaris. Second, the activities such as social mobilisation were not yielding very good results.

The programme achieved very good results in so far as the formation of groups was concerned. Beginning with 3 lakh groups formed in the first year, the total number of groups formed in a year reached more than 17 lakhs in 2003-04. There were 48.48 lakh SGSY groups in the country by the end of 2003-04.

Gradation exercise assumes importance in the SGSY programme as this seeks to gauge the development status of the group, rectify the weaknesses if any in the groups and pave the way for linkages with banks. The trends in the progress in the number of groups passing through the grades indicate the development status of the groups. Of the 48.48 lakh SGSY groups in the country, only 9.10 lakh groups (or only 25.74 per cent) passed grade I during the five-year period. This shows very slow progress in the grading process. The proportion of groups passing grade I in each year gradually declined. This suggests the following. First, the programme implementers were giving more emphasis to the formation of SGSY groups rather than their consolidation. Second, there seems to be inadequate capacity of programme implementers to prepare the groups to qualify for the grade I. Third, the co-ordination (among key actors such as DRDA, SGSY committee, banks, NGOs, etc.) required for grading was not present and hence, a huge gap between groups formed and groups passing through grade I. Even a smaller proportion of SHGs had passed grade II. Apparently, not all the groups passing grade II would undertake academic activities. The proportion of the groups undertaking economic activities to total SGSY groups was only 3.54 per cent. Thus, only a small proportion of SHGs undertook economic activities. It can be, therefore, concluded that although the progress in the formation of groups under the programme was impressive, a large proportion of them did not pass through Grade I or Grade II required to obtain assistance from the programme.

During the five-year period, 46 lakh swarojgaris obtained benefits from the programme; of them, most received benefits in their individual capacity rather than as group members. Thus, although the programme aimed to gradually shift to SHG mode, the emphasis was still on individual beneficiaries. Most of the assistance provided under the programme was used for agriculture related activities, in general, and for milch cattle, in particular. An analysis of the coverage of members belonging to disadvantaged and vulnerable groups shows that the programme achieved reasonable success, although the coverage of women was lower in a few states.

Micro Analysis

Any intervention on poverty alleviation requires a thorough understanding of the processes that generate poverty. In other words, poverty alleviation interventions will have good chances of success if they are designed on the basis of situation and needs of the poor. This implies that the SGSY programme, as per the design, should have enlisted the participation of the intended target group not only in the analysis of situation but also assessment of the needs. The needs cover the formation of groups, composition of the group, formulation of rules and regulations, etc.

The above brings out that social mobilisation was an important prerequisite before the group was formed. The intended target group should be provided with all the information on the programme, objectives, activities and the intended outcomes. The evidence presented in this chapter shows that social mobilisation process suffered due to fixation of target in the formation of groups, inability to train the facilitators, difficult conditions existing in the villages.

Participation of the people was not widespread in the formation of the groups, formulation of rules and regulations, meetings and savings contributions. Factors adversely affecting participation were widespread poverty, systems and procedures adopted in the groups, lack of incentives, inappropriate design and interference from village elite/influential persons. The limited participation of the people in the programme meant that the performance of the group was affected. Further, this also led to the tendencies of elite capture.

The evidence shows that the proportion of actual to mandated number of meetings was less than 100 per cent in a large number of cases. This means the inability on the part of the facilitators and representatives to hold the meetings as decided by the group. The facilitators from government departments, once the groups were 'formed' to meet the target, did not give much emphasis on the strengthening of groups as there was inadequate follow-up by higher officials due to problems of limited staff and lack of resources for mobility. The facilitators were also not trained in the consolidation of groups. In addition, the formation process was based on raising of expectations. When the facilitating staff from the government departments could not fulfil the expectations, they did not have the face or courage to meet the members. The attendance in meetings was also affected due to problems of limited livelihood opportunities, inconvenient meeting time, etc.

Limited participation in savings contribution meant that members did not have sufficient savings to borrow for meeting the urgent consumption credit needs, and for production. Small amounts of savings also meant that the vulnerability remained the outstanding problem for the poor. The differential amounts of savings contributed by members and savings linked to credit together implied that those having better economic capacity to save were in an advantageous position to borrow from the group and corner the benefits. This also implies 'elite capture'.

The analysis on participation of members in credit activities and undertaking of income generation activities shows that the programme had not succeeded in generating viable and locally suitable IGA. In both homogenous and heterogeneous groups, it was the influential groups of households which cornered the benefits.

But most often, the loan amount was invested upon already existing economic activities. For those who really thought of starting a new IGA, there were problems of skill acquisition and supply of inputs like raw materials. With the absence of linkages between groups, the GP and the line departments, collective mobilisation of people to identify economic activities was not even attempted.

Thus, participation meant costs for the poor. The SGSY programme has had limited success in explaining the benefits of the programme to the members, and convincing them that benefits would outweigh the costs of participation in the long run. The net result was a vicious circle of low participation leading to low participation, which, in turn, led to either dismally low levels of participation, exit of members from the programme and defunct of the groups.

The analysis of linkages among key development actors shows that there was a considerable bureaucratic control upon the entire implementation process. Although theory places heavy emphasis upon state and society linkages as being excellent catalyst for development, and despite the programme envisaging it in principle, it has not yet successfully achieved. Complementarity is expected to enhance sustainable synergy and development. However, the field data do not prove all this. First of all, it is premature to expect the decentralised bodies to undertake the task of establishing linkages with banks and other institutions. The PRIs themselves have not yet established firmly and independently as democratic bodies with power suitably devolved. The functioning of the groups is not the least transparent and have encouraged sufficient criticism and led to suspicions about their accountability. Although SGSY is open to all, our sample consists of only women's groups. In a way, this has shed light on certain special challenges for women's groups, given their illiteracy, restrictions on mobility and feminisation of poverty.

Inappropriate Functional Assignment

As per the Article 243G, the functions relating to women development and empowerment were to be assigned to Panchayat

Raj institutions. The guidelines of SGSY also note that the functions of formation of groups and monitoring and evaluation are to be assigned to PRIs. However, in practice this was not so. The programme implementation responsibility had been entrusted to the DRD on the assumption that they could utilise the secretary of the grama panchayat in the formation and consolidation of groups. The target of forming 320 groups in a block was considered stiff and the secretaries were insufficient in number, had heavy workload and thought to be lacking the required skills in forming SHGs. Hence, the grama panchayats were not pressed into service as far as the formation and consolidation of groups. This reflected that the programme violated the provisions of the 73rd Constitutional Amendment.

The assignment of key functions to the department of rural development proved to be inappropriate. With stiffer targets assigned, the department felt it necessary to divide the targets among several departments, and the departments of rural development, women and child development, adult education, agriculture, horticulture and veterinary were assigned the function of formation and consolidation of groups in the selected districts. The implementation function undertaken by the DRDA suffered due to lack of its own staff. At the block level, the executive officer had been assigned with the responsibility of forming the groups. Since the area to be covered was large, this functionary took the help of field level staff of various departments. While the department succeeded in meeting the targets on group formation, the quality of the groups suffered on account of lack of poor follow-up, inability to provide the departmental staff being exclusively meant for group formation and consolidation, and inadequate resources[1].

However, the executive officers mandated with the responsibility of supervising the groups were insufficient. In one of the selected blocks in Madhya Pradesh, five officials had to cover 160 villages; in another, four had to cover 140 villages. Given that these officers had to depend on public transport to undertake field visits, the mobility was restricted and the quality of groups suffered.

It was noted by the executive officers of taluk panchayats in the selected districts that between 5 and 60 per cent of SGSY groups across the selected taluks were not 'working' and were on the verge of becoming defunct due to these problems.

The key functions assigned to anganwadi worker also landed the programme into a problem. With a majority of the workers thinking that 'they were already overburdened with work', the functions relating to SGSY programme were considered to be an additional burden without any payment. Hence, the anganwadi workers thought the programme to be yet another poverty alleviation oriented one. The good governance principles included were not clear to them. Most of the higher level officers also did not explain these features. Prior to the formation the anganwadi workers were not provided with training on assessment of the situation and needs, participatory methodologies to be adopted in the formation of groups. All these adversely affected the quality of the groups formed, and the participation of the people also suffered. The influence of local elite was evident in the selection of households into the group and in the selection of office bearers.

Inter-governmental Transfers did not Produce Right Incentives

The function of releasing the matching grant was vested with the department of Rural Development. Yet, the grama panchayats were assigned with the function of monitoring and supervision of SGSY groups. Since the grama panchayats did not have to participate in decision-making with regard to selection of groups for the matching grant, they did not take much interest in the monitoring of the groups. In any case, only two out of 19 groups obtained external assistance. As the discussion on functions undertaken by the grama panchayats reveals, most of them did not play a significant role in the programme.

The programme also did not make sufficient provision towards paying honorarium to government staff involved in the formation and consolidation of groups[2]. Lack of monetary incentives to anganwadi worker meant that she did not take much interest in the consolidation of groups. Added to that she was not very well aware of the need to forge links with the grama panchayats. As a result, the performance of anganwadi workers in building the capacity of the groups in the linkage building was poor. Thus, the linkages between grama panchayats and SGSY groups did not work. And also, the mechanisms established to harmonise the relations such as SGSY committee at the block and district levels did neither address the issue nor functioned well.

Lack of Favourable Environment for the Linkages with the Banks

The banks were unwilling to extend credit facilities to SGSY groups because these groups were perceived to have come up to corner the subsidy 'by hook or by crook', and did not deserve a bank loan. Hence, the banks apparently delayed the process of gradation, and disbursal of loan even after a group obtained a good grade. The banks gave the reasons of limited staff in the banks and vast area to be covered by them as the reasons for the delay in the gradation process. The NABARD official stated that this was not the correct reason for the foot-dragging strategy adopted by the banks. The fact that most of the SGSY groups had either not been subjected to the grading process or not obtained bank assistance in the selected districts suggests that the linkages with the banks did not work.

Favourable Conditions for Micro-Finance

Micro-finance is widely regarded as an innovation having the potential to minimise risks in the credit market (Ghatak 1999; Ghatak and Guinnane 1999; Morduch 1999; Armendáriz de Aghion 1999). Micro-finance implies providing the poor with savings, credit and insurance facilities to set up or expand Income Generating Activities relating to agriculture, allied activities and non-farm sector, and thereby, increase household income security. Micro-finance services under SGSY programme are provided by a group of about 15 women members. The members periodically contribute savings, which are used to build a savings fund that can be revolved among the members. The members are encouraged to borrow from the savings fund, thus created, to meet their consumption and short-term production needs. Since this fund, built entirely on the savings of members, is normally insufficient to finance IGAs involving larger amounts of start-up capital, the micro-finance groups are linked to formal banks to obtain bulk loan for on-lending to group members.

The credit fund, if it comes from an outside source, is disbursed to individual members according to agreed criteria and the group undertakes joint liability for the debts of each member. Alternatively, funds may be lent to members individually, in which case the group jointly guarantees all the loans. The joint liability provides incentives or compels the group to undertake the tasks of selection, monitoring and enforcement of repayment in a cost-effective manner, leading to reduced transaction costs, increased volume of transactions and improved access of credit to the poor. For this to happen, the group should be small and homogenous, and have access to incentives[3] (Olsen 1965; Stiglitz 1990; Morduch 1999).

The knowledge on achievements of micro-finance is partial and contested. While one group of studies (Hashemi *et al* 1996; Puhazhendi and Badatya 2002) argues that micro-finance has very beneficial social and economic impact, others caution against such optimism (Montgomery *et al* 1996; Goetz and Sen Gupta 1996, Buckley 1997; Rogaly 1996; Mayoux 1998; Rajasekhar 2002a; Kropp and Suran 2002). Other studies suggest beneficial impact of micro-finance programmes; but argue that the micro-finance does not assist the poorest (Hulme and Mosley 1996).

This suggests considerable gap between theory and evidence (Morduch 1999), and calls for a discussion on problems involved in institutional implementation of joint liability lending in order to identify issues on roles of SHGs in enabling the poor to access financial services for income generation through self-employment activities.

Group Formation

The joint liability compels the micro-finance groups to be homogenous. This can be achieved by the group formation process which incorporates participatory methods to assess the situation and needs of the people interested in joining in the programmes (Sharma and Zeller 1997; Rajasekhar 2002c), practical measures in screening[4], and including persons who know each other and interact on regular basis.

However, the group formation in government programmes has become hasty and *ad hoc* as the task of forming the group has been assigned to poorly trained government staff having motivational problems (Rajakutty 1997). The same was true in the case of formation of SGSY groups. The inadequate staff, lack of training, inadequate incentives, target chasing, etc., contributed to less time spent to the group formation and lack of quality in the group formation process. As a result, the groups were heterogeneous. This raises the issue of whether government departments have qualitative human resources to form groups. This is perhaps an outstanding issue given that the programmes of the government allocate smaller amounts and time period for both human resources and for the formation of groups (Harper 2002). Given that the quality in the formation of groups is essential for ensuring the participation of members, the poor quality in the formation of groups implies that it was difficult for the programme to achieve good governance principles.

Savings Mobilisation

Micro-finance programmes enable the poor to save. Savings mobilisation (focusing on voluntary savings as well) has been emphasised in micro-finance programmes as savings provide an endogenous source of capital for lending. Savings also provide direct advantages to poor households such as building up assets to use as collateral, a reserve to reduce consumption volatility over time, improved access to consumption credit, reduced dependence on moneylenders and enhanced access to health, education, etc. This helps the poor to have confidence to invest on IGAs as the access to consumption credit frees them from uncertainties of how to meet consumption emergencies. The growing amount of savings improves the confidence among members in investing and expanding the existing income generation activities.

It was, however, found that the savings contribution was slow and irregular due to limited and insecure livelihoods, frequent migration (disrupting the life pattern of the poor), and inability of micro-finance group to provide the incentives. Further, inability of the groups to fulfil all the credit needs of the members may act as disincentive to the poor to contribute their savings to the group.

Do Micro-Finance Groups Improve Access to Credit?

Lending to a group member (by the group or external agency with the group providing joint liability) is less risky because of peer selection, which, in turn, takes care of problems posed by adverse selection. However, it has been emphasised that the access of the poor to credit tends to be limited (Rajasekhar 2002a). The present study has found that the SGSY programme did not improve the access to credit to members due to over emphasis on linkages with banks for obtaining resources and savings linked to credit. Even if some of the poor women wanted to undertake IGAs, their income earning opportunities were constrained by type (small, inaccessible and lack of marketing) of the villages, and social environment.

To sum up, the design of SGSY programme is good as it seeks further decentralisation and adoption of good governance principles. However, the programme implementation suffered on account of a number of problems such as inadequate functional assignment, inter-governmental transfers leading to disincentives and unfavourable conditions for income earning through micro-finance initiatives. Thus, bureaucratic attitude, limited decentralisation, lack of minimum development of areas and people contribute to the inability to follow good governance principles and decentralisation for income earning through employment generation.

NOTES

1. Acknowledging that these were the key problems, the CEO of one of the districts stated that (in the district level workshop) a decision to appoint temporary staff of motivator/facilitator to overcome this problem was recently taken. Further, he noted that Rs.2,000 were to be made available for each group for its consolidation.
2. Recently, a decision was taken by the state government to appoint facilitators for this purpose and pay an honorarium to the staff involved in the formation and consolidation of the groups.
3. These are savings linked to credit, disbursing a second and larger loan after the repayment of the first one, etc.
4. Wenner (1995) shows that direct screening of members according to their local reputation and adoption of a written internal constitution resulted in less default rates.

References

Armendáriz de Aghion, Beatriz (1999). On the Design of a Credit Agreement with Peer Monitoring. *Journal of Development Economics,* 60 (2): 79-104.

Bardhan, Pranab (2002). Decentralisation of Governance and Development. *Energy Policy,* 16(4): 185-205.

Bhalla, Surjit S. (2002). Growth and Poverty in India: Myth and Reality. In M. Govinda Rao (ed.), *Development, Poverty and Fiscal Policy: Decentralisation of Institutions.* New Delhi: Oxford.

Bird, R. M. (1993). Threading the Fiscal Labyrinth: Some Issues in Fiscal Decentralisation, *National Tax Journal,* 46(2): 207-27.

Bretton, Albert (1995). *Competitive Governments.* Cambridge: Cambridge University Press.

Brown, C. C. and W. E. Oates (1987). Assistance to the Poor in a Federal System. *Journal of Public Economics,* 32: 307-30.

Buckley, Graeme (1997). Micro-Finance in Africa: Is It either the Problem or the Solution? *World Development,* 25(7).

CGB (Cauvery Grameen Bank) (2000). *Credit Delivery Innovation by Cauvery Grameen Bank.* Mysore: CGB.

Chambers, Robert (1988). Poverty in India: Concepts, Research and Reality. *Discussion Paper 241.* Brighton: IDS.

Chambers, Robert (1995). Poverty and Livelihoods: Whose Reality Counts? *Discussion Paper 347.* Brighton: IDS.

Cornwall, A.(2002). Locating Citizen Participation, *IDS Bulletin,* 33(2): 49-58.

Datt, G. (1997). *Poverty in India and Indian States: An Update.* Washington: International Food Policy Research Institute.

DCO (Directorate of Census Operations) (1991). *Primary Census Abstract: General Population, Series-II, Part II-B (I), Census of India, Madhya Pradesh,* New Delhi: Government of India.

Dev, Mahendra (2002). Poverty in India: Trends, Macro-Policies and Direct Programmes. In M. Govinda Rao (ed.). *Development, Poverty and Fiscal Policy: Decentralisation of Institutions.* New Delhi: Oxford.

Dreze, J. and A. Sen (1989). *Hunger and Public Action.* Oxford: Clarendon Press.

DWCD (2000). *Annual Report,* 1999-2000. New Delhi: DWCD.

Etzioni, Amitai (1968). *Active Society: A Theory of Societal and Political Processes.* London: Collier-MacMillan.

Fernandez, A. R. (1993). *The Myrada Experience: Alternate Management Systems for Savings and Credit of the Rural Poor.* Bangalore: Myrada.

Ghatak, Maitreesh (1999). Group Lending, Local Information and Peer Selection. *Journal of Development Economics,* 60(2): 27-50.

Ghatak, Maitreesh and Timothy W. Guinnane (1999). The Economics of Lending with Joint Liability: Theory and Practice. *Journal of Development Economics,* 60(2): 195-228.

Goetz, Anne Marie and Rina Sen Gupta (1996). Who Takes the Credit? Gender, Power and Control over Loan Use in Rural Credit Programs in Bangladesh. *World Development,* 24(1).

GoI (1985). Evaluation Study of Integrated Rural Development Programme. *Programme Evaluation Organisation Study No. 134.* http://planningcommission.nic.in/reports/peoreport/cmpdmpeo/volumel/134.pdf.

GoI (1999). *Swarnajayanti Gram Swarozgar Yojana: Guidelines.* New Delhi; Ministry of Rural Development.

GoI (2001). *Report of the Working Group on Rural Poverty Alleviation Programmes for the Tenth Five Year Plan.* New Delhi: Planning Commission.

GoI (2002a). *Ninth Five-Year Plan, 1997-2002: Thematic Issues and Sectoral Programmes,* Vol. II. New Delhi: Planning Commission.

GoI (2002b). *Tenth Five Year Plan (2002-2007): Dimensions and Strategies,* Vol.1. New Delhi: Planning Commission.

GoI (2002c). *Tenth Five Year Plan (2002-2007): Sectoral Policies and Programmes,* Vol.II. New Delhi: Planning Commission.

GoI (2004). *Swarnajayanti Gram Swarojgar Yojana Guidelines.* New Delhi: Ministry of Rural Development. http//www. rural. nic.in/sgsy.htm.

GoMP (1998). *The Madhya Pradesh Human Development Report 1998.* Bhopal: Directorate of Institutional Finance, Government of Madhya Pradesh.

Gopalan, Sarala (2002). *Towards Equality — The Unfinished Agenda — Status of Women in India (2001).* New Delhi: National Commission for Women.

Harper, Malcolm (2002). *Promotion of Self-Help Groups under the SHG-Bank Linkage Program in India.* Bombay: NABARD.

Harry, Blair (2000). Participation and Accountability at the Periphery: Democratic Local Governance in Six Countries. *World Development,* 28(1): 1-30.

Hashemi, Syed M., Sidney Ruth Schuler and Ann P. Riley (1996). Rural Credit Programs and Women's Empowerment in Bangladesh. *World Development,* 24(4).

Hettne, Bjorn (1978). *Mobilisation and Development in India: A Case Study of Mysore State.* Stockholm: Swedish International Development Authority.

Hulme, David and Paul Mosley (1996). *Finance Against Poverty.* London: Routledge.

Joshi, S., M.K. Bhat and Edwin (1997). *Experience of Advocacy in Environment and Development.* Bangalore: DSI and NOVIB.

Kohkonen, Satu and Anthony Lanyi (eds.) (2000). *Institutions, Incentives and Economic Reforms in India.* New Delhi: Sage Publications.

Krishna, Anirudh (2003). Falling into Poverty: Other Side of Poverty Reduction, *Economic and Political Weekly,* XXXVIII(6):533-42.

Krishna, Anirudh, Mahesh Kapila, Mahendra Porwal and Virpal Singh (2003). Falling into Poverty in a High-Growth State:

Escaping Poverty and Becoming Poor in Gujarat Villages, *Economic and Political Weekly,* XXXVIII (49): 5171-79.

Krishna, Anirudh, Mahesh Kapila, Sharad Pathak, Mahendra Porwal, Kiranpal Singh and Virpal Singh (2004). Falling into Poverty in Villages of Andhra Pradesh: Why Poverty Avoidance Policies are Needed, *Economic and Political Weekly,* XXXIX (29): 3249-56.

Kropp, Erhard W. and B. S. Suran (2002). *Linking Banks and Self-Help Groups in India: An Assessment.* Bombay: NABARD.

Kumar, R. Gopa (1999). *Foreign Contributions to Voluntary Organisations in India: A Geographical Analysis.* New Delhi: JNU (mimeo).

Ladd, Helen F., Fred C., and Doolittle (1982). Which Level of Government should Assist the Poor? *National Tax Journal,* 35, September.

Mandhotra, Rohit and Shilpa Bhan (2003). *Self-Help Groups: The Functioning and Performance in Koshambi District of Uttar Pradesh,* Fieldwork Segment 2002-2004. Anand: Institute of Rural Management.

Mayoux, Linda (1998). Women's Empowerment and Micro-Finance Programs: Approaches, Evidence and Ways Forward. *Discussion Paper.* Milton Keynes: The Open University.

Montgomery, R., D. Bhattacharya and D. Hulme (1996). Credit for Poor in Bangladesh. In Hulme, D. and P. Moseley (eds.), *Finance Against Poverty.* London: Routledge.

Morduch, Jonathan (1999). The Micro-Finance Promise. *Journal of Economic Literature,* XXXVII: 1569-1614.

Narayanan, Pradeep (2003). Empowering through Participation: How Effective Is this Approach? *Economic and Political Weekly,* XXXVIII (25): 2484-86.

Oates, E. Wallace (1999). An Essay on Fiscal Federalism. *Journal of Economic Literature,* XXXVII: 1120-49, September.

OECD (2004). Decentralization and Poverty in Developing Countries: Exploring the Impact, OECD Development Centre Working Paper No. 236. Paris: OECD.

Olsen, Mancur (1965). *The Logic of Collective Action: Public Goods and the Theory of Groups.* Cambridge, MA: Harvard University Press.

Panda, Sudershan (2004). *Situation Analysis of NGO Involvement in Government Schemes' MTS* (PRM 2002-2004). Anand: Institute of Rural Management.

Paul, Samuel (1986). *Community Participation in Development Projects: The World Bank Experience.* A Paper Presented at an International Workshop Organised by the Economic Development. Washington: The World Bank.

Pauly, Mark V. (1973). Income Redistribution as a Local Public Good, *Journal of Public Economics,* Elsevier, 2(1): 35-58, February.

Puhazhendi, V. and K. C. Badatya (2002). *Self-Help Group Bank Linkage Programme for Rural Poor in India: An Impact Assessment.* Bombay: NABARD.

Rajakutty, S. (1997). Development of Women and Children in Rural Areas (DWCRA): Are We in the Right Course? *Journal of Rural Development,* 16(1): 85-112.

Rajasekhar, D. (1994). *Savings and Credit Systems of the Poor: Some Non-Governmental Organisation (NGO) Experiences.* Bangalore: NOVIB & HIVOS.

Rajasekhar, D. (1996). Problems and Prospects of Group Lending in NGO Credit Programmes in India. *Savings and Development,* 20(1): 79-104.

Rajasekhar, D. (2000). Non-Governmental Organisations in India: Opportunities and Challenges. *ISEC Working Paper No.66.* Bangalore: Institute for Social and Economic Change.

Rajasekhar, D. (2002a). Impact of Micro-Finance Programs on Poverty and Gender Equality: Some Evidence from Indian NGOs. In Shahra Razavi (ed.), *Shifting Burdens: Gender and Agrarian Change under Neoliberalism.* Bloomfield: Kumarian Press, Inc.

Rajasekhar, D. (2002b). *Savings Products for the Poor—A Demand Perspective: Results from Kamataka and Orissa.* A Report Submitted to GTZ/NABARD, New Delhi (unpublished).

Rajasekhar, D. (2002c). *Functions, Assets and Processes of LOs in Women Development and Empowerment Sector*. Bangalore: Decentralization and Development Unit, Institute for Social and Economic Change (mimeo).

Rajasekhar, D. (2004). *Poverty Alleviation Strategies of NGOs*. New Delhi: Concept.

Rajasekhar, D. and Narasimha Reddy (1997). *Local Government Programmes and NGOs*. Bangalore: DSI.

Rajasekhar, D. and R. R. Biradar (eds.) (2004). *Reluctant Partners Coming Together? The Interface between Government, NGOs and People*. New Delhi: Concept Publishing Company.

Rajasekhar, D. and Vinod Vyasulu (1990). The Rural Credit Delivery System: A Study in Pali District in Rajasthan. *Economic and Political Weekly,* XXVI(39): A-125-A-134.

Rajasekhar, D., B. P. Vani and K. G. Gayathri Devi (2004). *Role of Local Organisations in Women Development and Empowerment: A Study in Karnataka and Madhya Pradesh States, India.* Bangalore: Institute for Social and Economic Change (mimeo).

Rao, V.M. (2002). Eradicating Poverty: Some Missing Policy Dimensions. In M. Govinda Rao (ed). *Development, Poverty and Fiscal Policy: Decentralization of Institutions.* New Delhi: Oxford.

Rao, M. Govinda and A. Das Gupta (1995). Intergovernmental Transfers and Poverty Alleviation. *Environment and Planning, C: Government and Policy,* 13 (1): 1-23.

Rath, N. (1985). 'Garibi Hatao': Can IRDP Do It? *Economic and Political Weekly,* XX(6): 238-46.

Rath, N. (1990). 'Garibi Hatao: Can IRDP Do It?' In K. S. Krisnaswamy (eds.) *Poverty and Income Distribution,* Sameeksha Trust, New Delhi: Oxford University Press.

Reddy, Narasimha and D. Rajasekhar (1996). *Development Programmes and NGOs: A Guide on Central Government Programmes for NGOs in India.* Bangalore: BCO and Novib.

Robinson, M. (1993). Governance, Democracy and Conditionality: NGOs and the New Policy Agenda. In A. Clayton (ed.),

Governance, Democracy and Conditionality: What Role for NGOs? Oxford: INTRAC.

Rogaly, Ben (1996). Micro-Finance Evangelism, Destitute Women and the Hard Selling of New Anti-Poverty Formula. *Development in Practice, 6* (2).

Rutherford, Stuart (2000). *The Poor and Their Money.* New Delhi: Oxford University Press.

Satish, P. (2001). Some Issues in the Formation of Self-Help Groups. *Indian Journal of Agricultural Economics,* 56(3): 410-8.

Sen, Prabal Kumar, Haribandhu Panda, Harekrishna Mishra, Praddyut J. Modi and Kameshwar Choudhary (2002a). *Impact Assessment Study of Rural Development Programmes in Kalahandi District of Orissa.* Sponsored by the Ministry of Rural Development, Government of India (Monitoring Division), Anand: Institute of Rural Management. (unpublished).

Sen, Prabal Kumar, Haribandhu Panda, Harekrishna Mishra, Praddyut J. Modi and Kameshwar Choudhary (2002b). *Impact Assessment Study of Rural Development Programmes in Bolangir District of Orissa.* Sponsored by Ministry of Rural Development, Government of India (Monitoring Division), (unpublished), Anand: Institute of Rural Management. (unpublished).

Sharma, Manohar and Manfred Zeiler (1997). Repayment Performance in Group-Based Credit Programs in Bangladesh: An Empirical Analysis. *World Development,* 25(10).

Shylendra, H. S. (2004). The Emerging Governance Paradigm and Its Implication for Poverty Alleviation and Equity. *IRMA Working Paper No. 182.* Anand: Institute of Rural Management.

Stiglitz, J. E. (1990). Peer Monitoring and Credit Markets. *The World Bank Economic Review,* 4 (3).

Sud, Nikita (2003). Experience of SGSY in Gujarat: From Process-Oriented Theory to Deterministic Practice. *Economic and Political Weekly,* 38(39): 4085-87.

Todaro, Michael (1977). *Economic Development in the Third World*, New York: Longman.

Trond, Vedeld (2001). Participation in Project Preparation: Lessons from the World Bank Assisted Projects in India, *World Bank Discussion Paper 2001*. Washington DC: The World Bank.

Von Braun, Joachim and Ulrike Grote (2002). Does Decentralization Serve the Poor? In Ehtisham Ahmad and Vito Tanzi (eds). *Managing Fiscal Decentratization*. London : Routledge.

Uphoff, N. (1989). *Approaches to Community Participation in Agriculture and Rural Development*. Washington DC: The World Bank.

Webster, Neil and Lars Engberg-Pedersen (2002). *In the Name of the Poor: Contesting Political Space for Poverty Reduction*. London: Zed.

Weinberger, Katinka and Johannes Paul Jutting (2001). Women's Participation in Local Organisations: Conditions and Constraints, *World Development*, 29(8).

Wenner, M. (1995). Group Credit: A Means to Improve Information Transfer and Loan Repayment Performance. *Journal of Development Studies*, 32(2): 263-81.

World Bank (1996). *India: Five Years of Stabilisation and Reforms and Challenges Ahead*. Washington DC: The World Bank.

World Bank (1997). Staff Appraisal Report on Rural Women Development and Empowerment Project. *Report No. 16031-in*, *South Asia Country Department II*. Washington DC: The World Bank.

Index